PRINCIPLES OF SECURITY CONSULTING

Published by
American University & Colleges Press™
An imprint of American Book Publishing
http://www.american-book.com
Salt Lake City, Utah,
Printed in the United States of America on acid-free paper.

Principles of Security Consulting

Designed by Karen Maryanski, design@american-book.com

Publisher's Note: *This publication is designed to provide accurate and authoritative information in regard to the subject matter covered. It is sold or distributed with the understanding that the publisher and author is not engaged in rendering legal, accounting, or other professional service. If legal advice or other expert assistance is required, the services of a competent professional person in a consultation capacity should be sought..*

Library of Congress Cataloging-in-Publication Data is available upon request.

ISBN 1-930586-79-5

Read, Charles B., Principles of Security Consulting

Special Sales

These books are available at special discounts for bulk purchases. Special editions, including personalized covers, excerpts of existing books, and corporate imprints, can be created in large quantities for special needs. For more information e-mail orders@american-book.com.

PRINCIPLES OF SECURITY CONSULTING

An Introduction to Professional Security Consulting

Charles B. Read, Jr.

Dedication

To the heroes of September 11 and those who follow.

Foreword

In business, if customers don't trust you to maintain confidentiality, don't feel comfortable approaching and communicating with you, or believe you are anything less than completely objective in your thoughts and actions, they will not support you, no matter how great your product or service may be or how effectively it's marketed. We quickly learned that security in any form is, as Charlie Read says in this book, "as much a perception as it is a reality" and begins with acceptance by the individual employee.

Without the support of customers, be they internal or external, our products and services would never be accepted, or be effective. If only the phone companies were so customer-service focused!

The same holds true for security consultants. Consultants should be selected based on successful track records, not merely the contents of their marketing packages. Look rather at the personality and practical experiences they bring to the contract and how well they integrate with your program, your employees, and your team of experts.

Consulting of any sort is a specialized field in which the consultant may be viewed as a third-party expert or welcomed into the security team as its newest member. Indeed, the range of work environments and client-side relationships the consultant faces is diverse, and the consultant must be prepared to operate anywhere inside that range of environments. Remember, you have to be comfortable with the consultant working in, or representing, your office to your customers!

Throughout *Principles of Security Consulting,* Charlie Read prepares the reader for establishing professional security consulting credentials. His approach takes the reader from a historical foundation to modern-day security services and systems. He shares with you proven security surveys that, if followed, provide a detailed map sure to guide you effectively in conducting virtually all physical security consultations. His style is designed to have you, the future security consultant, think and act unconventionally regarding security matters.

Too many professional certifications and training centers emphasize security as a proactive process designed to support a reactive process following an adverse event. As such, the security mentality is almost always defensive rather than preventive and is frequently clouded by the comfort of defending the known terrain of the organization's information, buildings, people, and policies.

Unfortunately, as clearly demonstrated during the terrorist attack of September 11, 2001, the adversary' s thought processes are rarely in line with the established norms and policies of your company. Being able to think like the adversary helps strengthen any security program and goes a long way in separating a good consultant from a great consultant.

Ensuring alarm systems are installed and functioning might be on the good consultant's to-do list, but the great consultant will check to see what happens if the phone lines or power for the building are severed. Will the alarm still function, send a distress call to its central monitoring station, or simply go silent? How will (or does) the alarm company respond to such situations?

The good consultant will make sure that employee access cards are properly coded to only allow access where the bearer is authorized; but the great consultant will monitor critical areas to see if employees hold or prop doors open for other people to enter, whether employees check identification for people not using their cards to enter such areas, and how often and by whom the access lists for such areas are updated.

These are simply a few unconventional items that don't appear in the training materials offered by many security schools and professional certification programs. It is knowledge and wisdom gleaned from operational experience, not just books or classroom learning.

The adversary does not think conventionally and is not constrained by corporate policies and procedures. It is the successful adversary that exploits such conventional corporate thinking (and resulting security posture) to his advantage. Thus, the only way to implement effective security is for the security teams—and their consultants— to be able to think unconventionally in their analysis of such threats. That is why military special operations units are charged with anti-terrorism missions. They think and operate unconventionally, asking "why not" instead of settling on knowing "why." Consultants should maintain their perspective on the situation when planning a security program. Get information from multiple sources, such as colleagues, associations, and law enforcement entities, and not just the media or vendor-produced material. Ultimately, you' ll have a much more effective and manageable security program, one that actually works.

As you read through *Principles of Security Consulting*, keep in mind that Charlie Read is a security professional with significant experience in developing and managing security programs from an unconventional point of view, both as a special operations officer in the military and now as a civilian consultant. His significant operational career experience and unconventional approach to security is coupled with a down-to-earth training and writing style that presents a fantastic, readable, and relevant text on what it takes to become not just a good security consultant, but a great security consultant. After all, security is a state of mind.

Richard F. Forno, Chief Technology Officer, Shadowlogic
Washington, D.C. Author of *Incident Response* and former Senior Security Analyst, U.S. House of Representatives.

Preface

Charlie Read has written an excellent book dealing with the basics of security consulting. He has drawn upon his extensive experience in the security business to set out everything you need to know but were afraid to ask because you should have known it already. A very important part of the book is Chapter 14, which is entitled "Total Quality Consulting." In this chapter Charlie deals with a subject that is all too frequently overlooked by security professionals. Security people sometimes see themselves as the organizational police who have the right to make and enforce rules. Fortunately, those people don' t last long in the security industry because they don't get what Charlie calls "repeat business." The successful security consultant realizes he or she is dealing with customers, not someone seeking wisdom from on high. The successful consultant attempts to understand his client's business and organization and what role he or she can play in the success of that organization. This applies whether the consultant is doing a facility security survey, conducting an investigation, or advising a client on security equipment. Organizations and clients are different. One size does not fit all. Certainly there are accepted security standards. It is the consultant' s job to implement them to the client and his organization in such a way that security safeguards rather than hinders the business. Charlie also discusses the thought process you need to be a successful consultant. You need to remember you are running a business. While you certainly need to have a professional competence in security, you also need to understand your business. You need a vision and a plan on what you want your business to be and how you are going to get there. He points out that you need a mission for your organization. What are you going to be: a full service security consultant or a specialist in surveys or maybe investigations? Does your organization have the competency and skills needed to fulfill your chosen mission? As Charlie points out, feedback from your clients and treating customers as if they are important to your organization will give you these answers. Certainly no professional book today would be complete without a discussion of ethics. We tend to take ethics for granted. We think that business wants to do the right thing. But in the days of Enron and Arthur Andersen, we can no longer think that way. These cases show us that today, just as throughout our history, there are many people who will compromise their ethics and what they know is right for the almighty dollar. Just as important, these cases show that those who do compromise won' t succeed. In the first part of this work, Charlie does an excellent job of thoroughly and completely discussing the technical aspects of security that a good security consultant or student of security must know. His discussions are complete, but easily readable. Throughout this part of the book he weaves in the thought that a security consultant must be a business partner with his client. He continually emphasizes that security is to support the mission of the business and he shows you how to find the know-how and tools to do this. Charlie's book is well written and easy to read. It will be an essential reference for the student and well-seasoned practitioner alike. Edward F. Cunningham, Vice President Global Consulting, Brinks, Inc.

Contents

Chapter One

The History of Security Services

Introduction

Man has always attempted to provide for his safety and security. He developed weapons, built barriers around his dwellings, and devised codes of conduct to protect property and welfare—what we today refer to as laws, rules, and regulations.

Archaeologists have documented man's repeated attempts to protect or separate himself from others. Ancient dwellings have been uncovered where houses, and even entire villages, were constructed on lakes (for security), similar to dwellings still found in parts of Africa and the Far East. Cave dwellings demonstrate that early man utilized his natural environment for security. Several ancient cities have been uncovered to reveal high walls that surrounded entire towns. The Great Wall of China, now a Chinese national treasure, was built centuries ago to keep out the Mongols. Medieval European castles were encircled by moats and connected to land by drawbridges. Here in the United States, the historic movement westward required the construction of forts to provide security for the early settlers from hostile forces.

Man has used his ability to innovate and adjust to changes in the environment to provide safety and security. These needs were first addressed individually, then by communities at large. Customs, cultures, and relationships expanded beyond the family until the informal activities of early man became the formal rules, regulations and programs of complex societies.

Early European Developments

Early crude attempts by man to provide for the security of his family eventually evolved into formal, sophisticated safety and security programs when families began to form tribes or clans. Tribal security customs developed from this rudimentary system, which provided security for both the individual and the group. The Anglo-Saxon leader, Alfred the Great, was the first ruler to provide for the national security. The European feudalistic society was based on kinship and the relationship between an individual and his landlord. Kinship philosophy required the kindred to seek retaliation and restitution for an act against a relative. The landlord-tenant philosophy was a bilateral, although unequal, arrangement whereby the landlord would protect his servant from outside forces, and in return the servant would till the land to provide the necessary sustenance for life.

In 1066, William, Duke of Normandy, invaded and conquered England. William then instituted and implemented a national system that provided for collective, or community, security at the expense of individual freedom. William placed England under martial law and divided the country into fifty-five military districts. He placed an officer in charge of each district. This was the beginning of centralized responsibility for maintaining the peace and subsequently replaced local security programs.

In 1116, Henry II, son of William, Duke of Normandy, issued the Lieges Heroic in which he entitled himself the "Law Giver." The Lieges originated the idea of a distinction between those crimes judged to be serious, or felonious, and the lesser offenses deemed to be misdemeanors. This early English law was a forerunner of our present-day crimes classifications.

In 1166, the Assize of Clarendon revived the Anglo-Saxon system of mutual security, or frankpledge. This section of the code and the section dealing with trial by jury established an important tradition in the legal system of England.

In 1215, King John, a despised ruler of England, was forced by the barons to sign the Magna Charta. This document established a clear separation between local and national government and established the principle that the king was subject to the law.

In 1285, the Statute of Winchester reestablished a formalized law-enforcement system throughout England. This document required that all of England implement a security force, which was specified according to time, place and number of personnel. Duties and responsibilities were prescribed for those providing security and established punishments for those who disobeyed.

From approximately 1500 to 1800, the various communities of England were policed by a fragmented system of constables and watchmen. The first police officials were the sheriff, and later the parish constable. Parish constables were charged with maintaining law and order and were responsible to the justice of the peace. Because there was no authority coordinating this system, justice was fragmented and often of inferior quality, resulting in a great deal of corruption within the system. Justices of the peace were appointed by the Crown and were unpaid. These officials were usually selected from among the gentry. They frequently used their positions to serve their own needs and maintain the status quo by enforcing the laws in favor of their own social class.

In 1737 King George II began to pay watchmen from revenue from taxes collected specifically for security protection. Previously they were paid privately for their services.

The Eighteenth Century

Eighteenth-century England experienced an almost total breakdown of the constable system of law enforcement. The Industrial Revolution saw the beginning of rural populations moving to the cities to find jobs. Textile machines and new methods of metal production resulted in enormous industrial progress and the creation of many new jobs.

Production increased dramatically, yet there was also poverty and suffering among masses of people. Crime grew at alarming rates as the displaced, the poor, and the disenchanted grew in number.

Primarily because of their low caliber, constables and watchmen were unable to cope with the problem. It was difficult to recruit constables because of their poor reputations and equally poor pay. Constables often consorted with undesirables and were frequently themselves criminals who would only bring criminals to justice if the reward were adequate. Accordingly, little was done to curb lawlessness.

In 1748, Henry Fielding became Chief Magistrate. Before Fielding, crime and riots were handled by the militia. When a crowd became sufficiently destructive, the militia suppressed the riot. Fielding, however, developed a plan to thwart the criminals by actively investigating them.

Fielding realized that "citizens might combine together collectively, go out into the streets, trace the perpetrators of crimes in their haunts and meet the instigators of mob gatherings before they had assembled a following and caused destruction." He saw that it was possible to prevent, instead of suppress, crime and disorder. This contrasted completely with the constables who could not be found when trouble erupted.

Fielding formed a group of volunteers who arrested numerous criminals in the Bow Street area. These early detectives became known as the Bow Street Runners, and their success was well known throughout London. In 1752, Fielding started publishing *The Covent Garden Journal* to circulate crime news.

Although Fielding's efforts had great effect in the Bow Street area, his program was not applied throughout the city. Crime continued to be a major problem, and society's only solution to crime was the ineffective Constable system. Fielding's proposal to have paid magistrates with a preventative force of paid Constables went unheeded.

In 1796, Patrick Colquhoun published *A Treatise on the Police of the Metropolis*. The book detailed the crime problem in and around London. Colquhoun estimated that losses from various forms of theft, coining, forgery, and swindling amounted to a staggering $2,000,000.

He called for the formation of a large police force to combat crime in London. In 1785, William Pitt introduced a bill in Parliament that resembled Colquhoun' s plan. Pitt was met with a tremendous protest, however, and he was forced to withdraw his proposal. The citizens adamantly opposed the formation of a formal police force. People feared that the government would abuse such a force to spy on the people, infringe upon their liberty, and possibly aid in the formation of a totalitarian government.

However, Colquhoun did get a chance to implement some of his ideas. In 1798, some West Indian planters and merchants asked him for suggestions to alleviate the problem of massive thefts from ships and the London docks. Area merchants, with the approval of the government, financed the organization. A river police force was started with 80 permanent and 1,120 part-time officers. The police not only watched and patrolled the docks, they also participated in the loading and unloading of cargo. The experimental police department was a success. Savings as a result of the reduction of thefts was estimated to be $66,000 in the first eight months. The government assumed control of the department in 1800 and operated in until 1829 when it was incorporated into the Metropolitan Police Department.

The Peelian Reform

In 1822, Sir Robert Peel became Home Secretary. He had a strong belief in creating a unified, professional, and strong police force. Previously, when serving as Secretary for Irish Affairs, he reformed the Irish Constabulary, whose members were thereafter referred to as "Peelers." In his position of Home Secretary, Peel introduced the criminal law reform bill and reorganized the Metropolitan Police, also referred to as "Peelers," or better known as "Bobbies." Peel also attempted to decentralize the police forces and hold each community responsible for its own security.

Not all of Peel's efforts were successful. Neither the Police Act of 1835, establishing city and borough police forces; the County Act of 1939, creating county police; nor various other acts passed in the mid 1800s created adequate police operations. Use of private guard forces continued for recovering stolen property and providing protection for private persons and businesses.

Despite this, it was Peel and his vision that served as the model for law enforcement agencies for years to come, not only in England, but also in the United States.

During Peel's first few years in office, he concerned himself primarily with social reform. First, he consolidated the laws dealing with theft and the destruction of property into one volume. Then he did the same thing with all laws dealing with offenses against persons. In England at this time there were more than 200 offenses bearing the death penalty. Peel abolished more than a hundred of these. Benefit of Clergy, in which a clergyman could escape punishment for a first offense in certain felonies, was also abolished. Peel's reforms made it easier to prosecute sexual offenses by changing the rules of evidence.

In 1828, Peel appointed a select committee to study the police, and on July 27, 1828, they issued their report. The report called for the formation of an Office of Police under the Home Secretary, and all magistrates without bench duty would report to the Home Secretary. All police, constables, and watchmen would be incorporated into the Office of Police. The City of London was not included in this structure, aiding its acceptance by Parliament.

Peel appointed Sir Charles Rowan and Sir Richard Mayne as the first commissioners for the Metropolitan Police. Rowan was selected for his military background, and Mayne, a former magistrate, was probably selected because of his legal background. One of their first actions was to prepare a book of general instructions detailing the constables' duties and responsibilities.

One of Rowan and Mayne's important contributions was the list of nine principles that guided their department. These "standing orders" are familiar to anyone who has served as a policeman or security officer here in the United States:

1. To prevent crime and disorder, as an alternative to their repression by military force and severity of legal punishment.
2. To recognize always that the power of the police to fulfill their functions and duties is dependent on public approval of their

existence, actions and behavior and on their ability to secure and maintain public respect.

3. To recognize always that to secure and maintain the respect and approval of the public means also the securing of the willing cooperation of the public in the task of securing observance of law.

4. To recognize always that the extent to which cooperation of the public can be secured diminishes proportionately the necessity of the use of physical force and compulsion for achieving police objectives.

5. To seek and preserve public favor, not only by pandering to public opinion, but by constantly demonstrating absolutely impartial service to law, in complete independence of policy and without regard to the justice or injustice of individual laws; by ready offering of individual service and friendship to all members of the public without regard to their wealth or social standing; by ready exercise of courtesy and good humor; and by ready offering of individual sacrifice in protecting and preserving life.

6. To use physical force only when the exercise of persuasion, advice, and warning is found to be insufficient to obtain public cooperation to an extent necessary to restore order; and to use only the minimum degree of physical force which is necessary on any particular occasion for achieving a police objective.

7. To maintain at all times a relationship with the public that gives reality to the historic tradition that the police are the public and that the public are the police; the police being only members of the public who are paid to give full-time attention to duties which are incumbent on every citizen in the interest of community welfare and existence.

8. To recognize always the need for strict adherence to police executive functions, and to refrain from even seeming to usurp the powers of the judiciary or avenging individuals or the state, and of authoritatively judging guilt and punishing the guilty.

9. To recognize always that the test of police efficiency is the absence of crime and disorder, and not the visible evidence of police action in dealing with them.

Rowan and Mayne focused on a system of policing in which the police were partners with the public. They knew that the survival of their new police system was dependent upon the public's acceptance. They emphasized cooperation, justice, equality, and crime prevention. The "new" Metropolitan Police represented the first modern police force in history.

Initially, many opposed the establishment of the Police Department. Hostility toward the new police ranged from brutal murders of the newly appointed constables to public denunciation by judges, magistrates, and cabinet members, the public, and, on occasion, by King George IV himself. Frequently, the Constables were referred to as "Peel's bloody gang" and "blue devils." Ultimately, it was through the efforts of Rowan and Mayne that the police system succeeded. They impressed upon the officers the need to be courteous at all times and use physical force only as a last resort. Their policies minimized negative interactions with the public.

By June 1830, the force consisted of about three thousand men. Between 1829 and 1831, over eight thousand men had been enrolled, and over three thousand had been discharged for unfitness, incompetence, or drunkenness. Police brought about a reduction in crime, control of riots, and established order in London. The police concept was extended to the boroughs in 1835 and incrementally to the counties in stages from 1839 to 1856. Gradually, it spread throughout the British Empire.

Early American Police Development

Security practices in early days of colonial America followed the colonists from England. The need for mutual protection in a new and unfamiliar land brought them together in groups much like those of earlier centuries.

The Massachusetts Bay Colony installed the Office of Constable, whose duties included "keeping the peace, raising the hue and cry, controlling drunks, and apprehending criminals." By 1658, constable duties included "informing the Magistrate of new comers, taking charge of the Watch and Ward, tallying votes in general court, summoning jurymen for duty, bringing accused before the court, bringing before the court men and women not living with their spouses, collecting taxes, and other sundry duties, including the hanging of sheep-killing dogs where the owners refused to do so themselves."

As settlers moved west in Massachusetts, along the Mohawk Valley in New York into Pennsylvania and Virginia, they were faced with a need to protect themselves from hostile Indians and settlers from other nations, such as the Spanish and French. Their settlements usually consisted of stockades and forts surrounded by the farms of its inhabitants. When the alarm sounded the threat of attack, people left their homes and farms for the safety of the fort, where they joined in its defense.

Security of people and property in established towns followed English traditions. Sheriffs were elected in Virginia and Georgia. Constables were appointed in New England, and watchmen were hired to patrol at night. As the small colonial settlements developed into cities, night and day watches appeared. In 1631, Boston established a night watch, and in 1643, a burglar watch was established in New Netherland (New York). In 1700, Philadelphia established a night watch in which all citizens were required to take their turns.

During the early stages of these city programs, many watchmen took the job as a means of earning a second income. Most pursued regular occupations during the day and worked for the city at night. No standards existed, except those of a political nature, for the selection of personnel. One Matthew Young was appointed watchman in Boston "in order that he and his children do not become town charge." An investigating committee of the Board of Aldermen in New York made the finding that the incumbents were selected for political opinions and not for personal merit. Term of service by the incumbent was uncertain and often brief, depending on the change in political party. An 1838 investigation revealed that watchmen dismissed from one ward for neglect or drunkenness found service in another.

In 1844, the legislature of New York abolished the watchman system and created a police force. The act established a force of 800 men under the direction of a chief of police, who reported to the mayor. Boston followed New York's example and established a police force in 1854. Other cities soon followed suit

Establishment of new police forces may have solved some problems, but it also created new ones. From the beginning, most of the major municipal departments were embroiled in politics. The "spoils system" controlled the administration of many departments for most of the nineteenth century. This system of local governments caused many departments to deteriorate to nothing more than welfare systems of political patronage. Friends and relatives of politicians would be appointed to management positions over more highly qualified candidates. In some jurisdictions, applicants could secure employment only through bribery. When politics changed, there was generally wholesale firing of police at all levels, and the new mayor would appoint his people into the police department to aid him in controlling the city.

America had failed to learn from England's mistakes. During the last half of the nineteenth century and the first decade of the twentieth century, the police became a tool of the politicians. Their primary function was to maintain the status quo. A decentralized police system developed that was corrupt and inadequate. The American police, in part, became a part of the criminal element, rather than being a force that controlled criminality.

Development of Private Security in the United States

The development of security forces seems to follow no established patterns except as a reaction to public pressure for action. Colonists settling in America brought with them the English system of government and its reliance upon mutual protection and collective responsibility. Dutch, Spanish, and French influence in the colonies was minimal. Most legal concepts and security practices stemmed from England.

Influenced by Peel, New York adopted his general principles in 1833 to improve police operations. However, most police departments across the country were inadequate. As a whole, police departments in the nineteenth century were inefficient, ill equipped, poorly trained, and corrupt. Failure of governments—federal, state, and local— to provide adequate safety and security spawned the development and growth of the first professional private security responses in the second half of the nineteenth century.

The Pinkertons

Allan Pinkerton is considered by most to be the father of private security in the United States. In 1855, Pinkerton, after serving as a "Copper" and as the Chicago Police Department's first detective, founded the Pinkerton Detective Agency. For more than fifty years, his agency was the only company providing security and investigative services throughout the United States. During the Civil War, Pinkerton detectives were engaged as intelligence agents for the Union Army. However, their primary employer throughout the early years of the company was the railroad industry. His detectives and investigators concentrated on catching train robbers and providing other security services for the railroads.

The Pinkerton Agency was successful because inadequate public law-enforcement agencies were unable to provide protection and security to private citizens and private enterprises. Because public police were limited by geographic jurisdiction, they were restricted when investigating and apprehending fleeing criminals. This limitation facilitated the growth of private security. Pinkerton and his detectives became famous as they pursued criminals throughout the country.

Within a few short years of its inception, the Pinkerton Agency was a thriving private security enterprise. The foundation was established that the provision of security and protective services could be provided by private enterprises in such a way that both the interests of government and private individuals could be served.

Railroad Security and Police

During the 1800s, many states passed legislation granting the railroad industry the right to establish a proprietary security force. In most cases, these forces were given full police powers for the protection of company assets. Additionally, the Federal Railroad Law mandated that railroad companies provide for the protection of passengers and freight. With the westward expansion, railway lines were extended into sparsely settled areas that had little or no public protection. Trains were subject to attack by Indians and outlaw gangs that robbed passengers, stole cargo, caused train derailments, and generally disrupted communications and railway traffic. The railroad police are the oldest, most highly organized segment of the proprietary, private security industry in the United States.

Electronic Alarms

In the 1850s, twenty-five years before the electric light, Edwin Holmes of New York City invented the electric burglar alarm. In 1858, Holmes began the first central burglar alarm operation, and by the latter half of the century, electric alarm protection for industry and business establishments in New York City was quite common.

Security Delivery Services

During the westward expansion of the 1800s, stagecoach lines provided passenger, mail, and courier service throughout the West. These stagecoach companies faced the same crime problems as the railroads. Wells Fargo and others were the forerunners of the armored car and courier services that are visible today. By 1900, Brinks had a fleet of some eighty-five wagons, transporting numerous materials, including payrolls and other valuable shipments that could not be safely shipped by any other means.

The Twentieth Century

By the turn of the century, an expanding economy fueled by increased industrialization, immigration, and labor organizations created conditions, along with increases in crime and criminality, responsible for the growth of private security. In 1909, William Burns, a former Secret Service investigator and director of the Bureau of Investigation, founded the Burns Detective Agency. His agency became the sole investigating agency for the American Banker' s

Association and grew to be the second largest investigative and guard service company in the United States. Until the founding of the FBI in 1908, Pinkerton and Burns were the only national investigative service agencies in the country.

The complexities surrounding World War I contributed further to the growth of private security. Espionage and sabotage became a potential threat to American industry and commerce. Security personnel supplied by private contractors were utilized to guard facility assets and operations.

Following World War I, private security activity declined, reaching a low point during the Depression era. Like the war that preceded it, World War II provided the impetus to rejuvenate the private security industry. In many instances, the federal government mandated that contractors employ comprehensive security measures to protect materials necessary to the war effort from sabotage and espionage. As a result of this heightened state of security, private industry became more aware of the role that plant security could have in the protection of assets and personnel.

Now in the wake of the terrorist attack of September 11, 2001, we see a resurgence of government-mandated private security programs.

Crime and security problems will continue to outgrow the capacity of public law enforcement agencies to provide the services needed to protect people and property. Accordingly, there will be an increasing reliance on the role and function of security and protective services. The development and expansion of private and public security services has evolved from the basic historical stage to include some of the most progressive operational and technological techniques of crime prevention, detection, and apprehension in use today.

During the past two decades, the growth rate of the private security industry has far surpassed that of public law enforcement. Studies show that since the late 1930s, several thousand new firms have entered the private security field. There are now more private security personnel than law enforcement personnel in the United States. History tells us that this trend will continue. Security will be a growth industry for the next several years, just as it was for the 1990s.

Factors of Growth and Guard Service Expansion

World War II was largely responsible for the growth of the security industry. At the end of World War II, a continual gradual growth of security services in both the private and public sectors was experienced. The value and contributions of security to both the private and public sector had been established. Several private security firms, such as Pinkerton, Burns, and Wackenhut, achieved tremendous growth during the '50s and ' 60s. Companies providing their own proprietary guard services experienced equal, if not greater, growth. Today, contract security guards and proprietary security personnel can be found in almost every segment of commerce, manufacturing, institutional services, and government.

Polls taken each year indicate that the fear of crime is a greater problem than the crime rate itself. Estimated figures on the extent of crime against businesses are staggering—in the billions of dollars. Although the crime rate is predicted to continue its decline, fear of crime is likely to increase. One need only read a newspaper or watch the six o'clock news to understand the perception of this nation' s crime problem. Security is nearly as much a perception as it is a reality. Without the belief that one is secure, security cannot totally exist.

Technological Advances

Technology has and always will play a major role in the growth of the private security industry. Even the lock, one of the oldest security devices, has evolved to combination locks, time locks, electronic locks, and access-control systems that incorporate the advanced technology of television and microcomputers.

Technology has greatly improved the quality of electronic equipment, including television, radios, communications, and other areas of electronics adapted and assimilated into electronic security devices and systems. The progression from vacuum tubes to transistors to integrated circuit technology has played a major role in the growth of the security industry. Today' s devices are smaller, lighter, more easily concealed, and far more dependable. Electronic security products and services comprise a sizable portion of the security market, and electronic security devices are an essential component of any security program.

It is incumbent upon the modern security professional to stay current on changes in electronic security technology. No single book is going to provide all the technological information and remain viable; technology simply changes too rapidly and too frequently. It is prudent for the security professional to study information and articles published in the monthly and quarterly publications of several outstanding professional security organizations. Additionally, attendance at their training seminars and participation in their certification programs is highly recommended. Many college and trade schools offer security, electronics, and building trades courses that serve to enhance the professional' s knowledge. Plan on attending the security services and equipment expositions to be aware of the latest in technology.

Rising Crime Rates

Although crime rates in many regions are declining, they remain of staggering proportions. Crimes against persons and property in recent years have instilled in many a constant fear of being victimized on the street, at work, and even in their homes. Without question, the crime rate, coupled with graphic depiction of crime by the news media, has contributed to the growth of security in the United States. Guard services and electronic alarm devices are now seen as ways to provide measures of security that would deter or detect crime and criminality and protect against personal injury and loss of property.

However, technology has also aided the criminal. In addition to personal crimes of murder, theft, rape, assault, etc., new crime techniques are being utilized to perpetrate criminal acts. Computer crime, credit card fraud, and other forms of white-collar crime are relatively new and frequently beyond the capacity for effective investigation by public law-enforcement agencies. These types of crime have often required more time and other resources not readily available to overextended police agencies. A need has been created for a new kind of security person capable of utilizing highly sophisticated investigative techniques and security measures.

Fueled by the rapid response and extensive exposure of the news media, many serious crimes have become more prevalent in recent years. Chief among these are terrorist acts, including skyjackings, political kidnappings, bombings, holding of hostages, etc. Many private companies, public institutions, and governments have chosen to initiate additional and often elaborate security measures to thwart such criminal acts.

Government Regulation

In response to a need for greater public safety, governments at all levels have enacted laws, rules, and regulations promulgating an increase in security programs. The Federal Bank Protection Act of 1968 mandated increased security measures and equipment for federal banks. Since January 1973, the Federal Aviation Administration has required screening of all air passengers and their carry-on baggage. These are just two examples of how government regulations have served to nurture the growth of security. In both cases, security personnel and security products are needed to satisfy the new standards.

Professional Development

Private security is moving toward greater professionalism. As the need for private security rises and as the complexities and sophistication of the criminal element increase, a bigger, better, and more professional assemblage of security experts will be called upon. Professional security organizations have been founded to provide representation, a voice, if you will, for the security expert. Additionally, these organizations serve to assist with training and other professional development goals.

One such organization, the American Society for Industrial Security (ASIS), has a membership of more than 25,000 security managers. Founded in 1966, its past and current membership is made up of security practitioners whose purpose is to advance and enhance the security profession. ASIS serves as a major spokesman for the security industry, and in recent years has focused on the need for advanced research in loss prevention, crime reduction, and advanced security education.

Other security organizations include the National Council of Investigation and Security Services, National Locksmith Association, the National Burglar and Fire Alarm Association, the International Fraud Training Institute, and others. The Lion Investigation Academy (LIA) of Bethlehem, PA under the direction of its founder, Detective Joe Allercia, is a pioneer in the training and formal education of Private Detectives. LIA is licensed by the PA Department of Education to confer upon its graduates an Associates' Degree in Specialized Technology.

Security has evolved into a diverse, sophisticated, and complex field. The traditional concept of the night watchman will no longer suffice. Instead, a new security person is emerging: highly trained, more highly educated, and better able to satisfy the growing intricacies of the security profession.

One such security training company to emerge is The Blackwater Training Center in Moyock, NC. This unique facility provides military, police, and private security special operators with a variety of special operations, special tactics, and special weapons training. So unique are their programs that Blackwater is a proprietary manufacturer and supplier of premier, custom-designed target and training systems. Blackwater staff and faculty are selected from this nation's most elite military and law enforcement organizations.

Modern Security Services

Over the past thirty years, administrators in many areas of our social, government, and economic system have recognized that all problems of disruptions, thefts, vandalism, assaults, and hijackings could not be solved through the traditional public police agencies. As previously discussed, the growing economy, increased crime rate, and greater exposure of criminal acts by the media has created a security need that the police agencies cannot handle alone.

Public police do not have the manpower to fully protect large businesses and industries, hospitals, etc. These private needs for security of property and persons have generated a demand for private guard, protective alarms, armored car, private investigative, locksmith, and security consultant services. High cost and inconveniences associated with numerous acts of unlawful conduct, coupled with loss of productivity by a workforce fearing crime, caused managers in such areas as transportation, commerce, health care, retailing, industry, government, and schools to look toward alternative means of protection.

Although private security has been around for decades in major companies and industries, security was foreign to most quasi-governmental and public institutions. Today's needs for increased security came as businesses expanded operations and undertook assignments requiring more protection. The proliferation of plaintiff lawsuits against businesses for alleged lack of safety and security has also added to the growth of the security industry.

Security Services

Security services are varied. In an ideal situation, they are custom-designed to meet the needs of the client. Thousands of people are employed in a number of private security organizations. Some perform limited security duties, such as receptionists and night watchmen assigned to lesser positions of responsibility and authority. Others work in highly specialized and complex fields, such as arson investigation and alarm services.

Regardless of their level of responsibility and expertise, security people are involved in the overall protective services of our nation and have a direct and important bearing on crime prevention and reduction. Accordingly, it is important that private security units work closely with the formal governmental units of law enforcement.

Guard Services

To the general public, the uniformed security guard seen at retail stores, industrial plants, office complexes, banks, hospitals, sports complexes, and governmental facilities is the most visible part of the private security industry. Some wear the distinctive insignia of that organization, while others wear the insignia of a private, contractual firm. There are two distinct types of guard services: contract and proprietary.

Contract Guard Services: In this situation, the guard personnel are employees of the contracting firm (vendor). Their duties and responsibilities, whether highly technical or mundane, are defined by the contract and administered by the vendor. Depending on the number of guards, contracted managers and supervisors may or may not be present onsite. Generally, management or supervisory personnel from the vendor are consulted for advice and assistance before any new program is implemented. Contract guard service is purchased from a firm outside the organization, generally for a rate-per-guard hour. Normally, rate-per-guard hour includes the guard's complete salary and benefits package, including tax and worker' s compensation requirements. Personnel representing the vendor generally initiate new security programs and modifications to existing programs. Security vendors may be large international organizations, such as Pinkerton or Burns, or they might be small and operate in limited geographical areas.

Proprietary Guard Services: Proprietary guard services, often referred to as "in-house" security, are security personnel in the employment of the organization being protected. Salaries and other benefits are paid directly to the employee rather than a contract vendor. Duties and responsibilities are defined and controlled by the organization, generally not by an outside agency. Managers and supervisors of proprietary security personnel should be considered part of the corporate management team and should be included in the corporate decision-making process of planning and implementing programs in the areas of security and safety. Unfortunately, this is not always the case. Sometimes, responsibility for security service comes under the domain of the personnel/human resources, facilities management, or other administrative division with little or no security expertise. Many proprietary security units are referred to as "plant protection" units because their duties include accident prevention and investigation, vehicular and pedestrian traffic control, clearance and escort of non-employees, and fire prevention and protection, as well as basic law enforcement within the facility.

Protective Alarm Services

Many corporate and professional office buildings, commercial enterprises, industrial operations, institutional facilities, and private homes utilize a wide variety of alarm systems and services. Intrusion detection alarms (burglar alarm), robbery alert alarms, fire detection systems, medical emergency notification alarms, environmental control alarms (high and low temperature warning), and other specialized alarms, often technically sophisticated, are installed, maintained, and monitored by many agencies throughout the country. Both big and small service companies provide alarm systems and monitoring. Installation, maintenance, and monitoring are sometimes subcontracted by the providing vendor. Alarm systems can be either proprietary or contractual; that is, they may be installed, maintained, and monitored by the user or by a contract agency. Some systems are purchased, while others are leased. There are three basic types of alarm systems:

- The Local Alarm System. This type is designed to sound an on-premise alarm, such as a horn, bell, or siren. It serves to deter intruders and to alert persons in or near the premises to an unauthorized entry attempt.
- Direct Police Connect. This system is not audible on the premises. Instead, a silent electronic signal is sent to the police department over telephone lines. Upon receiving the alarm, police can dispatch personnel nearest to the alarm site. Frequently, police issue a citation requiring payment for "false alarm" calls.
- Central Alarm System. This type of alarm system also utilizes the silent alarm signal and can be customized to send either silent or audible alarms within the facility. Instead of being monitored by police, the signal terminates at a remote central alarm station, which may be contractual or proprietary. Contract guards, proprietary guards, or the local police who are notified by the central station attendant may make response

to the alarms. These systems can also be used for medical emergency situations in which emergency medical personnel are dispatched along with or in lieu of police. With today' s technology, sometimes fire alarm systems will be mated to the security system, creating a redundant system for added safety.

Armored Car Service

Some of the private units of protection specialize in guarding and transporting cash, securities, gold, jewelry, or other valuables. These operations provide a specialized service, usually to the financial institutions. They service automated teller machines, collect cash revenues at assorted businesses, supply cash payrolls, and provide transportation-security solutions for commercial operations and others who must transport valuables from one location to another. Armored car personnel are usually armed and operate in multiple jurisdictions. This requires special firearms licensing allowing them to cross over state lines while armed. Some of the larger armored car companies are Brinks, Loomis Fargo & Co., and Dunbar.

Private Investigative Service

Private detective agencies, ranging from sole practitioners with local operations to multi-employee international corporations, offer their services to private citizens, attorneys, accountants, and commercial and industrial enterprises. Licensing requirements for private detectives and private investigators (PI) varies by jurisdiction. In most cases, a license and bond are required to work as a PI. Unfortunately, there are some states that still do not require licensing. Qualifications generally require the applicant to pass a thorough background investigation, be of good moral character, and possess requisite skills and experience. Private detectives perform a number of services, including criminal and civil investigations, financial and fraud investigations, due diligence, pre-employment screening, litigation support, loss prevention and recovery, workplace violence, corporate intelligence, and others. Attorneys who desire information relative to clients, witnesses, jurors, suspects, or opposing parties often utilize the services of a private investigator. Industrial and commercial concerns that desire credit information, background checks on potential and current employees, or information on competitors also employ private investigative services quite extensively.

Locksmith Services

Locksmiths provide a distinct and often complex and critical function in the security industry. Choosing the appropriate locking devices and keying systems to fit a specific application is often best accomplished by the trained locksmith. While locksmiths often can provide a needed security service, their skills are often underutilized. Most locks are manufactured by large, national companies and distributed by various types of retailers and suppliers, therefore are more often purchased through retailers and installed by general contractors or in-house maintenance personnel. Such persons often do not have the expertise and knowledge of security possessed by the professional locksmith. With the proliferation of electronic and other sophisticated locking systems, the locksmith should be included in the physical security design and installation team.

Security Consultant Service

Private security consultants are a relatively new addition to the security industry. Escalating crime rates and rapidly changing technology have created a need for specialists to accurately identify and solve security problems. These individuals usually have years of experience and can provide valuable assistance to professional, industrial, commercial, or institutional clients who desire outside assistance with security-related issues.

Specialized Areas of Security

Security services can be provided by either a private agency on a contractual basis or be an integral, operating component of the organization itself. In either case, security cannot function independently of the organization it serves. Numerous other private security services are available, including special security patrols, insurance investigation, and polygraph examination, among others.

To fully understand the varied applications of security services, one must look to the whole range of businesses, industries, and organizations in which security plays a vital role. The specific needs and problems of the entity being served should dictate the security services provided.

Transportation

In the United States, millions of passengers and billions of tons of cargo are processed by the various transportation agencies each year. In New York City alone, over three million passengers ride buses, subways, and railroads each day. Every component of the transportation system has common and unique security problems.

Governmental or quasi-official agencies, airport authorities, port authorities and other mass transit agencies operate from a different legal position than most facilities owned and operated by a private enterprise. Generally, security employees of airport authorities, port authorities, and some mass transit agencies have the same law enforcement authority as a regular police officer of that jurisdiction.

In fact, many are police officer-vested with full law enforcement authority. As previously mentioned, railroad companies had the first large-scale, organized police forces in the country. Proprietary security guard employees of a contract security firm doing business as a private enterprise venture do not have the same power of arrest as a police officer of a particular jurisdiction.

Generally, unless deputized, commissioned, or provided for by an ordinance or state statute, private security personnel possess no greater legal powers than any other private citizen. However, due to the position occupied by security officers, they have much greater opportunity to use their citizen's power than does an ordinary citizen. This justifies considerable attention and training in the laws of the local jurisdictions.

Airports and Airlines – Air cargo thefts and passenger checks are the major security problems faced by airports and airlines. Several federal agencies have direct security concerns with airports and airlines, including the U.S. Customs Service, FAA, U.S. Postal Service, FBI, and others. Prevention and detection programs are in place to identify smuggling, terrorism, postal violations, illegal immigration, importation of non-inspected foods and plants, and other public safety concerns.

Most airport authorities have police departments and proprietary security forces to perform security functions associated with the properties of the airport. Additional requirements fall on the airlines themselves. The FAA has regulations requiring airlines to provide security in their respective locations in an airport. As demonstrated by the horrific attacks of September 11, a problem unique to airports and airlines is the potential for large-scale disaster. Terrorist acts and plane crashes are examples of events for which security personnel must be prepared. After the events of September 11, Congress hastily enacted legislation transferring several airport security responsibilities to the FAA.

Railroads – The railroad police are perhaps the oldest and best-organized segment of the private security industry. Railroads pay their security personnel salaries and fringe benefits comparable with other railroad employees or municipal police departments. Accordingly, railroad police agencies can attract and keep an excellent security force. Crimes against persons, thefts, sabotage, and vandalism are the industry's major security problems. Today, operating pursuant to federal and state laws, railroad police generally have similar law enforcement authority as state and local police, and many have law enforcement powers in more than one jurisdiction.

Maritime – Many large cities have a maritime authority that operates under governmental or quasi-governmental authority, and many large city police departments have marine patrol divisions, as do several state police organizations. The United States Coast Guard and United States Customs Service also have a law enforcement presence in ports that serve the international and interstate markets. Individual companies who lease facilities from the maritime authority often use a combination of proprietary and contract security services. Cargo theft and smuggling are among the major security concerns associated with the maritime industry.

Trucking – A majority of the materials and goods transported in the United States are transported by common carriers rather than by company-owned transportation fleets. Most materials and goods are transported by truck. Trucking firms generally rely on a small proprietary security protection force to deal with major thefts. They often utilize the services of contract security firms at fixed locations, such as terminals or distribution centers. Cargo theft, internal (employee) theft, product diversion, and hijacking are the trucking industry's major security problems.

Transit Authorities

Transit authorities, such as the Chicago Transit Authority and the New York City Transit Authority, are generally governmental or quasi-governmental agencies that are financially supported by both public funds and revenues generated by passenger services. Of their numerous concerns, the loss of revenues as a result of fear of crime and resultant decreases in ridership is probably the largest.

Robberies and vandalism are two major security problems. Additional concerns are similar to the rest of the transportation industry. Improvements in technology, hardware, and architectural design are the latest improvements to benefit the transit systems. Transit authorities are seeking to increase visibility in passenger waiting areas, reduce patron waiting time, and provide quick detection and response to criminal incidents through better utilization of technologically advanced hardware, improved communications, specialized architectural design, and more efficient deployment of security forces.

Commerce

Commercial facilities have unique security problems not easily solved by current police practices. Police agencies have neither the manpower nor the capacity to provide security services for the vast number of financial institutions, hotels, or other commercial enterprises in the United States. These businesses cater to the general public and must encourage a feeling of openness and availability if they are to remain competitive. At the same time, businesses must project an image of safety and security. Commercial facilities must provide for protection against an array of criminal activities, from the simple theft to complex schemes to defraud. They must always put the safety of patrons and employees first.

Lodging

Similar to transit authorities, facilities managers must make their customers feel secure from crime. The security problems associated with the hotel and motel industry are usually related to the crime patterns of the surrounding area. The most frequent security problems associated with the hotel-motel industry are thefts from automobiles and guests' rooms and vandalism to the property of both the facility and guests. Other concerns facing hotels is their use by undesirable persons and the commission of vice-related criminal acts, including gambling, prostitution, and drugs.

Generally, security services are provided by a proprietary staff supplemented by employees of a contract security firm. A security manager is usually the decision-maker, and the contract employee performs the patrol function. Again, the use of technologically advanced hardware and efficient architectural design aids in providing for the safety and security of hotel guests.

Office Buildings

Large commercial office buildings typically have elevator banks in the lobby area and security personnel who control most of the pedestrian traffic from one central location. Frequently, visitors are required to register with a guard prior to gaining access to the elevators. Closed circuit television (CCTV) systems are in common use throughout office buildings. They are often found in elevators, freight docks, public-space (lobbies and passageways) points of access and egress, and other public areas where individual privacy is not violated.

Contract security personnel generally provide security; however, some building owners and building management firms do employ proprietary guards. Security guard duties include monitoring the CCTV and making regular security checks throughout the building, screening visitors, etc.

The major security problems for commercial office buildings include after-hours burglaries and thefts, internal thefts, fraudulent "slip and fall" insurance claims, loitering, and trespass. Within the past few years with the advent of the small laptop computers, office complexes in metropolitan areas have experienced large-scale theft of the computers during the business day. Frequently, thieves gain unauthorized access by "piggybacking" behind legitimate personnel during periods of high pedestrian traffic. Dressed in business attire or disguised as service or delivery personnel, they seek unattended, non-secured computers and other valuables.

CCTV systems properly positioned, monitoring both access and egress, can assist in the identification and apprehension of these thieves. Computer thefts are generally of two types: thefts for resale and profit and thefts to obtain proprietary business information, otherwise known as industrial espionage.

Financial Institutions

Financial institutions face security problems quite different from those of other commercial enterprises. In addition to several common indirect losses sustained by other businesses, most losses to financial institutions are direct financial losses. These losses vary from simple theft to complex fraud, embezzlement, and other criminal schemes. The sheer number of financial institutions, bank branches, and the proliferation of automated teller machines have grown at a rapid rate, resulting in significant increases in robberies, larcenies, burglaries, and vandalism.

In response, Congress passed the Bank Protection Act of 1968 requiring federally insured banks, savings and loans, and credit unions to designate someone to be a security officer, cooperate with and seek security advice from various law enforcement agencies, and develop comprehensive security programs and implement protection measures.

Credit card, check, and other financial frauds are also a major part of the fixed losses sustained by financial institutions. Local police, the FBI, and the Secret Service investigate crimes against financial institutions.

Health Care Institutions

Unique security problems face the health care industry. Hospitals, for example, must remain open to admit the sick and injured, to allow patients to have visitors, and to carry on the normal activities that are required in caring for those who are unable to care for themselves. This openness creates unique challenges in providing adequate public safety, physical security, and access control.

Hospital Security – By their very nature, hospitals attract people experiencing great emotional duress. Additionally, declining socioeconomic conditions, particularly in inner-city locations, has generated a tremendous need for greater security in hospitals. This decline of the inner cities has compelled hospital administrators to deal with the problems of security.

Previously, hospital administrators were not skilled in the area of security. Now, in most hospitals, the security duties are the responsibility of a professional security director and a security force. Smaller, private hospitals seldom employ a totally proprietary security force like those of major industrial corporations. Instead, they frequently utilize the services of contract security agencies to supplement their own security employees.

In addition to crimes generally associated with open facilities, health care institutions are also subject to the theft of controlled substances, prescription medications, high-value medical equipment, health insurance fraud, emotionally generated violence, and other unique criminal activities.

Nursing Homes – Nursing homes are full-service health care units for the elderly and severely disabled. Senior citizen residences offering limited nursing care and independent and assisted living facilities now exist in most major metropolitan areas. Medical needs and financial limitations are generally the determining factors in selecting these types of facilities.

Like hospitals, nursing homes and senior citizen residences are faced with the security problems of visitor control and internal theft. Robberies and burglaries are prevalent; with the elderly occupants of the nursing home most often the victims. The elderly are also frequent targets of fraudulent schemes. Many of the elderly are "soft targets" and, as such, there is an increased responsibility to provide for their safety and security. Restricted-access doors and CCTV are widely employed by nursing homes. Many nursing homes also engage the services of private contract security firms.

Retail

Retail stores are open, public-access facilities. Retail stores are a part of society in which the average citizen has direct contact with on a regular basis. Like any commercial endeavor, the more persons who come into contact with a particular facility, the more prosperous the business will be. Accordingly, retailers strive to create an environment that will attract shoppers.

Part of creating a welcoming atmosphere is creating a sense of safety and well being for the customer. Additionally, loss of merchandise by both internal and external theft is a major security problem associated with the retail industry. Frequently, the cause of lost merchandise is unknown. Retailing is a competitive business, and the loss of valuable merchandise has a direct and profound impact on profitability. In addition to CCTV and other technology, retailers frequently engage the services of store detectives, whose job it is to detect, apprehend, and prosecute violators.

Shopping Centers and Malls – Shopping centers and malls are constructed to provide numerous retail stores in one large complex. Generally, at least one large department store, known as an "anchor store," will dominate and is often the "drawing card" used to attract shoppers to the mall and the several small specialty shops in close proximity. Garages and open parking lots facilitate thousands of automobiles in and near the facilities.

This concentration of people and automobiles, coupled with public access in a small geographical area, creates numerous security problems. Shoppers will be deterred from shopping at stores where crime is a problem, leading to further losses of revenue. In many shopping centers and malls, CCTV is used to monitor pedestrian and vehicular traffic. Thefts from particular stores are usually handled by that store. Mall security departments are usually charged with protecting the common areas.

Recently, some police departments have added internal and external mall patrols to their duties, with some malls providing office space for the police to maintain a community-policing unit within the shopping complex. Cooperation among mall security, individual store security, and the police is critical to the success of public safety in malls and shopping centers.

After closing hours, fire watch and loss prevention are the primary functions of security personnel in a shopping center. Nationwide, there is a mixture of contract and proprietary security services in the retail industry.

Retail Establishments – Theft of merchandise is the single largest security problem facing retail owners. Losses due to criminal acts in the retail industry are almost twice that of other industries, such as manufacturing, wholesaling, services, and transportation. Shoplifting is the principal theft problem associated with most retail loss. Open merchandising techniques often provide the means for theft by emphasizing customer accessibility to merchandise.

Even though security personnel have been able to profile typical shoplifters and have made technological improvements in electronic detection and monitoring systems, shoplifting continues to plague most retail establishments. Internal theft by employees also accounts for significant losses in the retail industry. Losses due to internal and external thefts can equal or exceed the net profit of the business.

Most retail establishments operating on regional or national levels employ their own security forces. These employees have major responsibilities for loss prevention, planning, training, and implementing all phases of various security operations. Because of their similarities, security and safety services are frequently a joint responsibility.

Industrial

Regardless of size, industrial enterprises must protect the safety of their personnel and provide for the security of their inventory, facilities, and trade secrets. Many of the most innovative and progressive security practices are found in the area of industrial security, which is rapidly encompassing such activities as fire protection, traffic control, investigations, and the entire function of protecting life and property within an industrial enterprise.

Manufacturing

Like industrial facilities, manufacturers are varied in size and in the products they make. As in the industrial arena, manufacturers are required to provide for the safety and security of their personnel and to protect their facilities, products, inventory, and trade secrets. Security in the manufacturing industry is concerned with the theft of raw materials and finished products, and also with the physical security of installations, personnel, and classified information.

CCTV and a host of other technologically advanced security systems, while still engaged in some manufacturing facilities, are replacing the traditional "night watchman." This change has encouraged the development of the security manager position, whose duties include security, law enforcement, fire prevention, disaster recovery, accident investigation, public relations, and other areas of safety and security.

Public Utilities and Energy Companies

Utility companies are a vital part of the infrastructure of this country. Disruption to, or tampering with, the distribution of electric power, water, telephone, or other public utilities has the potential of being disastrous. We have witnessed terrorist acts in foreign countries in which public utilities were a prime target. Terrorist organizations have been able to immobilize major parts of cities, and the same potential exists in this country.

The bombing of the World Trade Center in New York should send a loud and clear message to the security professional. Sabotage of an electric generating plant or large substation would likely cause a major power disruption that could last for hours or even days. A damaged natural gas facility or a water facility could cause problems for a large segment of a city, especially during severe winter months.

Nuclear facilities have come to public attention with the nuclear accidents at Three Mile Island, Pennsylvania, and recent problem at Con Edison's Indian Point plant in New York. Potential accidents themselves cause major security problems, but the attention given to all nuclear plants is creating additional security problems that did not exist a few years ago. Environmental groups and ordinary citizens are demonstrating in large numbers against nuclear facilities in operation and under construction and are potential sources of criminal activity designed to create greater attention by the media and public. Terrorists, consisting of the "crazies, criminals, and crusaders" are among those whose potential to cause catastrophes requires public utilities to employ high-caliber security professionals.

The oil and gasoline crises of late 1970s brought national attention to the oil companies, and as a result, the federal Department of Energy now requires greater security for manufacturing facilities and storage areas. Energy manufacturing plants, storage facilities, and coal mining operations tend to be regionalized, and the resultant need for security is also regional in scope. Oil and gas manufacturing and storage facilities have the same basic security concerns and vulnerabilities as the public utilities.

Most oil companies are multinational corporations, and therefore are subject to worldwide security problems and terrorist threats. Kidnapping of executives for ransom has occurred in foreign countries and is potentially a major security problem today for American firms.

Special Events

In most major cities, private security plays a significant role in maintaining order and providing traffic control at special events, such as sports arenas, fairs, and amusement parks. Local law enforcement agencies often do not have the means to provide full-coverage security service for such events.

A relatively new approach has been taken by public law enforcement agencies in many urban jurisdictions. Organizations sponsoring special events often contract directly with police departments who, in turn, assign off-duty officers to police the event. These officers function in their full capacity as police officers and are paid regular salaries directly by the department, with the municipality being compensated by the event sponsors. On a national basis, a few contract security firms specialize in providing security services for all types of special events.

Civic Centers – Civic centers are multipurpose facilities that are usually owned or controlled by local government. Event security requirements are dictated by the nature and size of the events. Crowd control and other security services will vary depending on the type of event and the emotional state of the crowd. Sporting events, for example, generally require a lesser degree of security than perhaps a large heavy-metal rock concert.

However, in certain cities and during major playoff games, a higher degree of security may be needed. In response to problems with public drunkenness and disorderly conduct, Philadelphia assigns a municipal court judge to conduct arraignments in a lower-level office in Veterans Stadium. Security working in close cooperation with Philadelphia police, along with "instant arraignment" of suspected violators, has resulted in a significant reduction in criminal activity in the arena. A contract security firm generally has a contract with the civic center and provides security for all events.

Amusement Parks – Traveling seasonal carnivals are being replaced by huge amusement parks located throughout the United States. These facilities spread over hundreds of acres and are host to hundreds of thousands of vacationers every year. Depending on their geographical location, some amusement parks remain open all year. The need for the safety and security of visitors is paramount.

Security services include safety and accident prevention, vehicular and pedestrian traffic control, and prevention of vandalism and sabotage to rides and other equipment and facilities. The presence of thousands of visitors per day requires that the security force be capable of reacting to any contingency affecting the security of visitors or employees. Most amusement parks employ a proprietary security force.

Fairs and Exhibits – Exhibit halls and public fairs are often open throughout the year. Security requirements for each event are dependent upon the type of function and the number of people attending.

At most events, security needs include crowd control, parking, traffic control, and maintaining order. However, at certain events, such as jewelry shows, art exhibits, or antique shows, loss prevention is the primary concern. During idle times, burglary, theft, and vandalism are concerns that might justify employing a full-time security force. Most large fair and exhibition centers utilize proprietary security services and may supplement coverage with contract guard forces.

Government

The security of government buildings, parks, wetlands, Indian reservations, and monuments, to name a few, is a huge task. Protection must be provided for thousands of acres of land and buildings located throughout the United States. The vast number of government buildings and holdings makes it impossible for regular law enforcement units to provide service sufficient to satisfy all the demands for security.

Many governmental agencies, such as the General Services Administration, maintain large proprietary security forces consisting of both sworn law enforcement personnel and civilian security guards and security advisors. State and local governments often employ small proprietary law enforcement and security staffs or utilize a contract agency.

Security problems for government lands and buildings include the full spectrum of crimes against persons and property. Security is a full and equal partner with the other services required to operate government buildings and facilities.

Government Buildings – The General Services Administration (GSA) is charged with managing, operating, maintaining, and protecting federal buildings and related real estate and personal property. GSA operates the Federal Protection Service (FPS), a law enforcement agency of approximately five thousand personnel. Federal facilities not under the control of GSA usually maintain their own law enforcement or security personnel; examples are the U.S. Park Police, U.S. Park Rangers, uniform division of the Secret Service, and others.

Federal law enforcement and security officers are required to attend a service training academy and regular in-service training courses. Federal police have the same powers of arrest as regular police officers while on federal property under their control. The contract guards have only the powers and authority of a private citizen.

Most states have similar security forces with law enforcement or security responsibilities for state-owned, leased, and occupied buildings and property.

Public Housing – In large metropolitan areas, housing authorities were established and high-occupancy housing units built to provide housing for low-income persons. Development of high occupancy, multi-unit apartments in relatively small geographical areas immediately created numerous security problems. Housing authorities are generally governmental or quasi-governmental and have a proprietary security force, many of which are police departments or divisions of large city police forces. Their powers of arrest are the same as the regular police force for the jurisdiction.

The Department of Housing and Urban Development (HUD) has funded numerous low-income, private-housing projects that often contract service firms to handle their security services. Housing police and security departments must provide full-service law enforcement and security services to these often crime-infested projects.

Schools

Colleges, universities, and now public and private primary schools face serious threats to public safety. Accordingly, many employ well-organized, full-time public safety and security departments comprised of high-quality personnel. The size and quality of school public safety organizations has increased steadily over the past decade.

Primary Schools – It seems that almost daily we learn of uncontrollable horror stories and security problems at public and private schools. Vandalism and violence has become so extensive that administrators have assigned teachers regular patrol duties. Recently, we have even seen the assignment of police officers to provide on-site school security. Even though safety of individuals is the primary concern of school safety officers, order maintenance and vandalism consume most of their time.

College Security – Colleges today, especially residential colleges, face the same crime and security problems as the communities surrounding them. Many private colleges employ professional public safety departments. Most public colleges employ security and public safety agencies consisting of both sworn and non-sworn personnel. The development of the campus security force has been largely determined by external factors. Modern transportation and the campus-building boom of the 1960s shifted the security office from a fire watch to a protective and control function.

Security Today

Americans are confronted with alarming rises in crime and a constant fear of crime. They are seeking services beyond the capacity of the nation' s over-committed and understaffed public law enforcement agencies. Accordingly, the number of private security personnel now exceeds that of public law enforcement, and the number and types of companies doing business in security products and services has increased dramatically along with the number of private businesses employing their own security forces.

The need to fight crime and provide for a safe and secure environment has resulted in the recognition of private security's potential for contribution to national crime prevention and reduction. Differing roles of the public and private security forces have, due to their very nature, created a distinction between the police and private security services. Police agencies are enforcement-oriented; that is, they usually act after a crime has been committed. However, private security primarily serves as a crime prevention or deterrence force.

While their orientations may differ, their goals are the same. Serving a common goal emphasizes the common interests of private security and the public law enforcement system. The private security sector cannot and was never intended to replace public law enforcement; instead, each component must communicate, cooperate, and coordinate with the other in an effort to control crime. Put simply, to be successful, public and private security must come together as a team.

The extent and complexity of our nation's crime problems dictate that the two components work professionally together without competition or disharmony. Increased professionalism in the private security industry will serve to upgrade existing practices and procedures and will result in greater acceptance by the law enforcement community. Higher standards, better training, and licensing requirements will increase the effectiveness of private security services and provide for a more mutually productive and beneficial relationship between public law enforcement and private security.

EXAMPLES OF ACTUAL CLIENT PROBLEMS SOLVED

Problem:

Two international professional/business service companies merged to form the single largest service organization of its kind in the world. Once formed, the Global Security Director was faced with determining what the "new" company actually had and what they needed to properly and uniformly provide security for over sixteen thousand employees located throughout almost every state in the country.

Solution:

Security Consultants performed comprehensive Security Site Surveys, averaging sixty hours each, at 153 facilities in cities nationwide. *Security Consultants* evaluated existing systems and equipment, audited security guard services, ensured Y2K compliance, performed risk analysis and threat assessments, coordinated with; architects, national, regional, and local directors of infrastructure, police and fire department personnel, building inspectors, and other professionals dedicated to public safety and security. *Security Consultants* provided an integrated plan for establishing uniform, corporate-wide physical security programs applicable to the size, geographical location, and functionality of each site within the United States.

Problem:

A female employee was being stalked and harassed at home and in the workplace by her domestic partner.

Solution:

Private Investigators coordinated the efforts of two municipal police departments and documented the illegal activities of the offender. Upon presentation of the evidence, police were able to secure an arrest warrant and apprehend the offender. The investigators assisted the victim and company Personnel Manager in obtaining a Court Order of Protection. Additionally, disparaging information about the victim, provided by the offender to the client company, was proven to be false and the employee's reputation and career saved.

Problem:

Building Management was advised that a high profile, former foreign Head of State would be speaking on their premises one day prior to the his arrival.

Solution:

Consultants met with Building Management Executives to review all issues relating to the situation. After initial consultation with management, they assisted with the preparation of an Operation Plan to include: Building security, monitoring of tenants and visitors, security assignments, building checks, emergency ingress and egress, emergency procedures, handling of protestors, technician responsibilities, parking and traffic, vendors, monitoring of cleaning crews, and deliveries. After the Security Procedures and Operation Plan was reviewed, a Physical Site Security Survey was performed and a Liaison was established with the U.S. Secret Service, Bureau of Diplomatic Security, and local law enforcement. The event occurred without incident.

Problem:

Building Management was advised that a World Trade Organization conference would be held within close proximity to their location. The WTO conference, when previously held in a western city, attracted more than five thousand protestors, resulting in rioting and significant destruction to property in the areas of the protests. Building Management was advised of the event only one week prior to its commencement.

Solution:

Consultants immediately met with Building Management and became the "Security Team" for Building Management throughout the duration of the event. Some of *consultant's* primary responsibilities were building security, monitoring of tenants and visitors, personal safety for Building Management, tenants, and visitors to the site, security assignments and briefings of security personnel, building checks, emergency procedures, protestor parking and crowd control, monitoring of work crews and inspection of delivery vehicles, and liaison with federal, state, and local law enforcement (approximately 400 officers on-site). Although arrests were made and property damage was incurred by other facilities, there were no incidents involving the client's facility or property. *Consultants* received commendations from both the Sheriff and Prosecutor's offices.

Problem:

Investigative Consultants were engaged by the CEO of a mid-size service company to determine if an employee had violated company policy regarding unauthorized personal use of the computer and LAN system.

Solution:

Working with the MIS and IT Managers, *Investigators* determined that the employee in question did in-fact violate company policy relating to computer usage. They further documented that the employee had accessed inappropriate "sexually explicit" sites on company property, during work hours, and discovered that the employee had accessed such sites several hundred times a day for at least one month.

In addition to his resultant lack of productivity, the employee put the company in jeopardy by having such offensive material serve as the catalyst for a potential sexual harassment complaint. Additional information was developed that indicated that the employee might be involved in illegal Internet activity. The case was successfully referred to high-level public law enforcement officials in a totally discreet manner, thus preventing embarrassment of the company by the employee's alleged illicit activity.

Problem:

Laptop computers, computer hardware, and personal belongings being stolen from several office spaces, on three floors of a Class-A office building in a major metropolitan city over a period of several months.

Solution:

Consultant instituted an investigative plan that included the installation of covert cameras. After coordination with the client, facility manager, city police and building security guards, *investigators* identified the perpetrators and notified police detectives when subjects reentered the building. Subjects were arrested without incident. One subject was a parolee and the other a fugitive wanted for a string of commercial burglaries. Both have extensive criminal records. Neither was able to post bail and both remained in custody on numerous counts of burglary pending trial.

Chapter Two

Threats and Risks

To appreciate the role of security in America, one must understand the tasks it faces. All threats to security can be classified into one of two broad categories: natural and man-made.

Natural Hazards

Risks relating to natural hazards present unique and difficult situations to manage. When natural disaster strikes, it also affects public safety, security, emergency, medical, and other professionals, as well as their homes and families. Some natural occurrences are, of course, more common to some areas of the United States than others. The following list represents some of the more common natural hazards and where they are most likely to occur:

- Earthquakes – Most common in the Pacific coast
- Tidal waves or tsunami – Most common in coastal areas.
- Floods – Most common in coastal areas and low-lying areas with natural or man-made waterways.
- Fire, lightning – Can occur anywhere in the U.S.

- Storms, hurricanes – Most common in coastal areas
- Tornados – Can occur anywhere in the U.S.
- Snow and ice – Can occur anywhere in the U.S. except in extreme southern areas
- High winds – Can occur anywhere in the U.S.
- Temperature extremes – Can occur anywhere in the U.S.

Modern climatology and meteorology has made many natural hazards more predictable. Often it is possible to have advance warning and some indication of the probable magnitude of a pending hazard. Unfortunately, natural hazards frequently strike without warning, and it is then that preplanning and immediate and adequate reaction capabilities are of the utmost importance. Contingency and protection plans for emergency personnel, facilities, and equipment must also be made. You can't respond if you lose your people and material in the disaster.

Although it is impossible to prevent natural disasters, there are steps that can be taken to minimize the loss of life and property. First, choose a site for the facility where such disasters are rare. Second, construct a facility that will withstand anticipated natural hazards. Third, develop emergency plans to reduce the damage that such disasters can do. Fourth, create mutual assistance programs so that others may be capable of responding to "your" problems. This will require cross training and the establishment of effective communications as well as other planning measures.

Man-made Hazards

Man-made hazards are either intentional or accidental actions. It is often difficult to ascertain if an occurrence was intentional, accidental, or the result of a natural phenomenon. Floods, for example, may result from too much rain in a short period of time, or be the result of an intentional or accidental act in the improper operation of flood control barriers.

The two most common and devastating types of hazards and disaster are fire and crime. Fire obviously can be the by-product of intentional, accidental, and natural occurrences. Crime, as we know, is man-made; criminal culpability in a particular situation will be determined through investigation and judicial decree.

Fire

Fire claims thousands of victims each year in the United States. Additionally, thousands more are injured, millions of dollars in property is damaged or destroyed, and severe losses of jobs, customers, employees, and businesses occur. The National Fire Protection Association advises "fire is more related to human acts of omission and commission than to science...there is no denying that people cause most fires, and that most 'people-caused' fires are due to thoughtless acts of carelessness than from any uncontrolled interactions of reactive materials."

Fire is most frequently the result of human acts or neglect, such as poor housekeeping, careless use of smoking materials, inadequate or improper construction, improper utilization and maintenance of equipment, and intentional acts of arson and sabotage. The human element in fire is far more prevalent than natural environmental influences.

As an integral part of the security service, fire prevention programs must include a comprehensive analysis of the hazardous materials and operations that are common to the environment within your areas or responsibility. Disaster analysis must be used in developing effective fire safety rules and regulations.

Most fires are the result of human error and, therefore, are frequently preventable. Discipline, training, and education are the keys to fire prevention. Fire safety and prevention programs beginning in preschool, elementary, and secondary schools and continuing to the workplace are essential. Safety programs, including drills and training should be mandatory for ALL employees of an organization. No one, regardless of position within the organization, should be exempt from being fully informed of the importance and techniques of fire safety. Rules and regulations regarding fire safety should be common knowledge to every employee, and these standards should be strictly enforced.

The threat of fire cannot be totally eliminated. A threat of fire remains even with exhaustive preplanning, education, and training. Accordingly, a realistic goal of total prevention of fire in addition to establishing comprehensive emergency response plans must be sought. Fire is a real and major adversary capable of causing enormous destruction, losses, hardships, pain, and human suffering. Security duties include preventing and controlling fire. Training, education, evaluation, and inspection are areas in which security, therefore, plays a vital role.

Crime

Crime is among the key principal threats facing all Americans. In order to detect and deter crime and criminality, we must understand its intensity and know the threat environment, the criminal, and the roles society plays in its occurrence and prevention. Crimes are divided into two basic types: crimes against persons and crimes against property. Crimes against persons include murder, kidnapping, rape, assault, and robbery. Crimes against property include burglary, arson, vandalism, sabotage, shoplifting, and theft. Crimes are also classified in their severity as misdemeanors or felonies. A misdemeanor is usually defined as a crime with a penalty of a fine, a jail sentence of up to a year, or both. The penalties for a felony range from fines, one or more years or in prison, or the death penalty.

General Descriptions of Crimes

- Crimes – Felonies and misdemeanors. Lesser infractions, i.e., violations and offenses are NOT crimes.
- Robbery – The forcible stealing or taking of something of value from the custody or control of a person by force, threat of force, or by putting that person in fear of his or her welfare.
- Burglary – The unlawful entry or remaining in a building or structure to commit a crime therein, even though no force may have been used to gain entry.

- Theft – The unlawful taking of property or the receiving of stolen property or something of value without the use of threat, violence, or fraud.
- Arson – The willful, malicious burning or bombing of a dwelling, building, or other property with or without the intent to defraud.
- Vandalism – The intentional or malicious destruction, injury, or disfigurement of property.
- Fraud – An intentional misrepresentation to induce another to give up or part with something of value or to surrender a legal right.
- Shoplifting – The removal of merchandise from a store with the intent to deprive the owner of his property without paying the purchase price.

The means by which crimes are perpetrated are varied and complex. It is the responsibility of the security professional to become familiar with the criminal statutes as they apply to his/her responsibilities. The security professional must reduce the risks of victimization by being aware of the factors involved. The security professional should be aware of how types of businesses, locations of business, types of merchandise, nearness and responsiveness of police protection, and types of protective hardware and procedures employed are instrumental in inviting or deterring criminal attacks.

There will always be some deviant behavior in society. However, crime can be reduced if effective and efficient measures are taken to deter and detect crime or deny access to those activities that are detrimental.

The Criminal

Criminals are not readily identifiable by their appearance, speech, manner, background, attitude, behavior, skills, or method of criminal operation. There are, however, some factors that can be utilized to identify the criminal and deter or thwart his or her attempts to commit a crime regardless of personal characteristics.

There is no such thing as a "typical" criminal. Each person acts and reacts according to his or her own inherent and acquired characteristics and capabilities. The security professional must be aware of his or her surroundings, have a thorough knowledge of the elements of crime, and understand the various modus operandi or methods of operation (MO) employed by criminals.

The primary objective of most criminals is personal or financial gain. Accordingly, theft-related crimes are the most frequent and account for a good deal of the prevention and detection responsibilities of the security professional. Less common criminal activities, but of equal or greater concern, include the destruction of property and crimes against persons. These are considered the violent crimes.

Most criminals do not want to get caught and will avoid "hardened" targets to avoid apprehension. "Soft" targets of opportunity for robbery, burglary, and other crimes exist where it is readily apparent to the criminal that his goals are easily attainable, victims are relatively unprotected, and that there is little danger of being detected or apprehended.

Although some professional, or career, criminals earn a living from criminal activity, most crimes are committed as "crimes of opportunity" by amateurs, most of whom are juveniles and youthful offenders. Criminologists estimate that professional criminals account for only a small percentage of the total criminal population. Professional criminals make their living usually through one specific crime that has become their specialty. The professional likely began his career as an amateur, but was able, through luck or perhaps intelligence, to develop his skills to the point of being a "successful" criminal. He usually develops a distinctive and refined modus operandi by which he can frequently be identified.

Given the time and proper conditions, a highly skilled and determined professional criminal can successfully penetrate nearly any protective system. Therefore, in addition to deterring the criminal, it is of great importance to distract, inconvenience and interfere with his progress. The longer it takes a criminal to perpetrate his crime, the more vulnerable to detection and apprehension he becomes. When this threat becomes too severe, the criminal will be deterred and most likely will seek softer targets. Facilities well secured by strong locks and other perimeter barriers, effective lighting, and protected by alarm systems and CCTV will deter most criminals, whether amateur or professional.

To effectively protect his property, the security professional must view his belongings as though he himself were a criminal looking for a target and as the detective investigating the crime. The views from the criminal's and investigator' s perspectives should reveal both the weaknesses and the strengths of existing security measures. The security professional should have knowledge of the methods and techniques utilized by criminals to commit crimes if effective countermeasures are to be taken.

It is sad but true that many criminal activities are initiated from within the environment to be protected. The "internal threat," is represented by the employee requiring owners and security professionals to evaluate protection needs from both within and without. Statistics show that losses each year due to employee crimes are much greater than those committed by external sources.

Conclusion

To be complete, security must be approached systematically. Analyzing the threats, whether internal or external, man-made, or natural, is the mandatory first step in providing effective preventive or deterrent action.

Recent developments in detection and alert systems along with technological advances have made it possible to receive warnings of many probable or actual hazardous conditions. With in-depth planning and adequate preparation, property losses and life-threatening events can be reduced.

Current crime statistics indicate that social and cultural problems of the most serious proportions threaten the safety and security of all people, homes, and places of business in the United States, as well as Americans traveling and working abroad.

Chapter Three

Protecting the Perimeter

The ability to protect and secure any facility or building largely depends upon the environment or general location of the structure. The area immediately surrounding the facility must be secure if the facility itself is to remain secure. The first line of physical defense is the perimeter. It is here that we most desire to deter the criminal and prevent intrusion. The effective employment of alarms, access systems, CCTV, barriers, lighting, the security design of the structure itself, and the posting of guards accomplish perimeter security.

The more accessible a facility is, the more vulnerable it becomes. As security measures are increased, vulnerability decreases with resultant increases in cost to management and inconvenience to employees, patrons, and management. Efforts to secure a facility perimeter largely depend upon why it is being secured and frequently create a "balancing act," requiring tradeoffs in terms of the quality and quantity of security with regard to costs, inconvenience, and aesthetic qualities. The selection and deployment of security services and personnel are, therefore, usually dependent upon the perception of costs, needs, and utility of action.

Site Layout

Frequently, security is the last concern or is even totally disregarded during the planning and construction stages of a facility. Management and real estate divisions are often more interested in other requirements, such as location as it pertains to easy access, tax incentives and other issues, economy of construction and operation, and convenience. Sometimes, it is only after construction has begun or the facility put into operation that management considers security.

In some instances, security technology isn't even included in the building's blueprints or other specifications. By this time, the security problems are much harder to address. It is not uncommon to see perfectly good, brand new construction demolished or modified to facilitate the installation of security systems because security was an "afterthought." To properly, effectively, and efficiently provide security, security specialists should have input from the initial architectural planning stages through building completion. This will facilitate appropriate compromise of cost, convenience, and security issues. If adequate attention is not given to security during the planning stages, then overall security costs fueled by losses, injury, and inefficiency, will probably increase and are likely to outweigh any earlier perceived savings.

Security planning begins with site layout and the positioning of the facility on the building lot. Care should be exercised to ensure that the building or buildings receives maximum exposure from adjacent thoroughfares. The more isolated a building is, the more vulnerable it will be to unauthorized access and egress.

A Law Enforcement Assistance Administration (LEAA) study showed that in over two-thirds of the burglaries reported in selected areas of California, the points of entry were not visible. Likewise, robberies increase in locales with limited visibility. Would-be robbers tend to select targets in areas where they are likely to avoid detection.

When feasible, it is generally best to situate a building in the middle of the lot to facilitate movement around the facility and aid in observation. When this is not possible and a structure is located adjacent to another structure, additional security measures must be taken to protect against unauthorized access and egress.

With proper planning, installation, and maintenance, landscaping should also play an important role in crimes. Desires to make the facility as attractive as possible can be balanced with security needs. The introduction of shrubbery, trees, and other vegetation or ornamentation must be carefully planned. Without the proper consideration, landscaping can compromise security. If possible, the size and placement of vegetation should be located fifty or more feet from the structure. This will increase visibility and help deter illegal activities by eliminating or limiting the concealment of would-be perpetrators.

Planning and care should also be taken with regards to where and how equipment, products, supplies, and materials enter and leave the facility. These areas should remain free from obstruction to decrease the possibility of employees or carriers secreting goods and merchandise and later retrieving them. This is especially important around loading docks, mailrooms, and rail entrances.

"Hardscaping"—ornamental fencing, lighting, fountains, etc.— is an integral part of landscaping that is used to beautify and, when properly planned, can be of benefit to the security program. Frequently, management uses lighting for advertisement without regard to security. Security lighting and fencing are addressed in separate chapters.

To be efficient and cost effective, security planning should be early and continuous throughout the construction process. Structures and perimeter areas should not only be pleasing to the eye, but also designed and constructed to reduce their vulnerability to illegal activity.

Physical Barriers

There are two basic types of barriers: natural and man-made. Natural barriers include geographical obstacles such as rivers, lakes, mountains, cliffs, deserts, canyons, swamps, or other types of terrain. Natural features have been utilized to serve as primary or secondary security barriers since the beginning of time. When possible, natural barriers should be part of every modern security design. Man-made physical structural barriers include fences, walls, grills, and bars.

When properly designed and used, both natural and man-made barriers can effectively accomplish the following security objectives:

- Define property boundaries
- Deter entry
- Delay and impede unauthorized access
- Direct and restrict the flow of persons and vehicular traffic
- Provide for more efficient and effective deployment of security forces

Perimeter Barriers and Protection

Perimeter protection is the first line of defense against unauthorized access and perhaps the last line of defense against unauthorized egress. The properly designed, installed, and utilized barrier is both a physical and psychological deterrent to unauthorized movement in and out of the facility.

An effective barrier deters thefts, intrusions, and vandalism. However, the perimeter barrier will not stand alone as a total defense, but must be supplemented with guards, alarms, CCTV, etc. Organizations relying exclusively on physical barriers for their security may be exposing themselves to crime that escapes detection by other means. Without additional security measures, some crime, such as internal theft, may go on for years without detection.

Walls and fences are the most popular physical barriers and can be constructed out of wood, stone, cement blocks, concrete, and other materials.

Fencing

Fencing is generally used to secure larger areas or "special security areas" within an already secured facility. The three most popular types of security fencing are chain link, barbed wire, and concertina wire. The type used depends on the permanence of the fence and the level of security needed.

Chain Link Fencing – Chain link fencing is attractive due to its clean, neat lines. It poses less of a safety hazard because it does not have barbs, yet the small openings still reduce intrusion. Chain link fencing is easily and inexpensively maintained and augmented with the addition of barbed wire and concertina wire.

When chain link fence is used, it should be constructed of No. 1 gauge or heavier wire, with its mesh openings no larger than two inches. When possible, chain link fence should be at least eight feet in total height. The fence should be topped with a "V" top guard (outriggers), or arm bars bent at forty-five degrees and three strands of barbed wire attached on both sides to inhibit unauthorized access or egress. Some building codes specify how and where the strands of barbed wire may be placed.

A newer variation of the barbed wire top guard is "razor wire," thin ribbons of extremely sharp metal on which are attached extremely sharp, pointed projections of metal. A fence should be permanently attached to metal posts set in concrete. When possible, the fencing should be buried at least two inches below the surface (this is especially true if the soil is soft or sandy), or a strong wire should be woven through the lowest sections of the wire mesh to inhibit attempts to go under the fence. Where the fence crosses rugged terrain, such as streams, hills, or ditches, precautions must be taken to ensure that there are no unprotected openings beneath the fence.

Barbed Wire Fencing – Except as an addition to the top of chain link fences, barbed wire is rarely used to secure perimeters due to its unsightliness and the danger of inflicting wounds on those who come into contact with it. When barbed wire is used to mark boundaries, it should be five feet high and consist of three to four strands tightly stretched, attached to posts that are from six to ten feet apart. Barbed wire is also useful in supplementing natural barriers on occasion. For example, barbed wire could be strung along the side of a cliff to further deter intrusions.

Concertina Wire Fencing – Concertina wire, barbed wire, and the newer "razor ribbon" come from the manufacturers rolled into coils and are clipped together at intervals. They can be used as a barrier to secure a perimeter. Concertina is most effective when one roll is laid on top of two other rolls or in conjunction to other fence types. A barrier height of approximately six feet is the most effective. When utilized, the rolls should be fastened together and attached to the ground periodically with ground stakes. Concertina wire is one of the most difficult barriers to penetrate.

Concertina wire is unsightly and hinders ground maintenance, and thus, it should not be used as a permanent barrier without appropriate planning. Placing it between two parallel chain link fences with a stone or gravel base, for example, will provide extensive security without ground maintenance problems. This type of installation is seen at high-risk, high-security facilities like prisons and classified government facilities. Concertina wire has several advantages and can play an important role in perimeter security. It can be laid and picked up rather quickly by a trained person with the appropriate tools and can be used as a mobile barrier in emergency situations. For example, if the permanent barrier, say a chain link fence, is damaged as the result of an accident or a tree falling onto the fence, concertina wire can be quickly laid to hinder intrusion until permanent repairs are made. It can also be used to temporarily block roads or paths in case of an emergency.

Barriers should be constructed in as straight a line as possible to prevent would-be intruders from hiding close to the fence. Obstructions and vegetation should be kept clear or trimmed within fifty feet of either side of the barrier to prevent the hiding of persons, burglary tools, or stolen property. Barriers should be examined regularly to check for obstructions and breaks in the barrier and to supplement the effects of the barrier itself. The frequency of patrols depends on the desired degree of security and should always be conducted after extremes in weather or indications of any threat against security.

Building Security

The second line of defense against unauthorized access and egress is the building itself. A perimeter barrier may not always deter the determined intruder. The design of the building and the use of other security measures should be engaged to assist in controlling access and egress. This is especially true where perimeter barriers are located in isolated areas.

Buildings can be intruded from six different directions: the roof (top), flooring/basements (bottom), or one of four sides. Efforts should be made to completely secure the exterior of a structure, but primary consideration is given to roof access, doors and entrances, windows, and miscellaneous openings, such as fire escapes, vents, or delivery and trash portals.

One of the most vulnerable sections of any structure is the roof. The roof, especially flat roofs, are difficult to observe, thus affording intruders ample time and concealment to make an entry, and roofs are generally constructed of materials that are easily compromised. When possible, roofs should be constructed of impenetrable materials with a high pitch, which makes them difficult to maneuver on and easy to observe from the ground.

The number of attachments to the structure (such as fire escapes) should be reduced, making it more difficult to obtain access to the roof. Finally, the area immediately surrounding a structure should be kept clear of obstructions so that it would be difficult to hide ladders, ropes, etc. When access is reduced, the possibility of illegal entry is also reduced.

Many unauthorized entries and exits occur through windows. Windows not specifically equipped with security features are probably the most vulnerable part of any structure. If possible, the number of windows should be reduced or window security equipment must be considered, especially for windows on the ground level.

Properly installed, the introduction of metal grates or bars over windows and intrusion detection alarms will assist in reducing the vulnerability of windows. Proper installation includes tamper-resistant steel connector bolts completely through the wall and connecting the bolts on either side with a piece of flat steel and nuts with lock washers.

Protective windows and window coverings are helpful in deterring the amateur criminal. With the addition of intrusion detection systems, window protection will also deter the pro. The Uniform Crime Reports (UCR) consistently point out the large numbers of burglaries and larcenies that are committed by juveniles or nonprofessional criminals.

Doors are also frequently used to obtain illegal access. Many are soft targets and are easily violated. Doorways should be well lighted and free from obstructions. Metal doors are best, and should be equipped, at a minimum, with both deadbolt locks and horizontal retaining bars. When a wooden door is used, the inside should be covered with sheet steel to prevent intruders from kicking in or cutting a hole through it. Whenever possible, retaining bars with local sounding alarms should be installed on all doors except those most often used.

Special design precautions must be taken when buildings adjoin other structures. When this occurs, it becomes possible to gain entry to a second building by knocking a hole through a common wall. This frequently occurs when a low-security structure adjoins a high-security structure containing valuables. The entry usually occurs during off-hours, weekends, and holidays, when intruders have the time and ability to work unnoticed. When this situation exists, security must either be supplemented with alarms, or design and construction-correction attention should be paid to the facility or adjacent structure.

Cooperative Issues

The security posture must be compatible with management and with the daily operations of the facility. The system must ensure maximum security, but at the same time, it must allow for normal entries and exits and facilitate the conduct of business. To be complete and comprehensive, the system must be coordinated with other activities, such as fire protection and plant safety.

Perimeter security is burdened with the regular comings and goings of employees and visitors. During the changing of shifts and peak traffic times, intruders can more easily pass into the facility undetected unless preventive measures are taken. When a facility has large numbers of employees, contractors, vendors, and visitors, it may be necessary to issue badges or identification cards. Badges and cards should be color-coded for ready identification of personnel and the nature of their presence. Access is then restricted to appropriate areas of the facility. Vendors and contractors, for example, seldom have a legitimate reason to be in certain executive areas. If there is a need for tight security, visitors should be required to make appointments or check in with a security guard before entering the facility.

When a business or facility maintains a perimeter barrier and provides parking, the parking area should be located outside the perimeter barrier. This segregation significantly reduces the chances that intruders will successfully enter the facility when they must first pass a security point on foot. Such an arrangement maximizes access control.

When management provides parking facilities, they should be adjacent to the perimeter barrier and guard posts. Parking lots should be well lit to facilitate observation over the facility. Panic alarm stations (blue light stations) should be considered to enable the rapid summons of security personnel. Additionally, the use of CCTV and employment of mobile patrols will complete parking lot security.

It is vital to control the access and egress of employees and visitors and also to control vehicular traffic within the facility. The fewer entrances there are, the easier it is to control the perimeter. Accordingly, only those entrances necessary to the facility should be opened. Perimeter barriers usually have primary entrances and secondary entrances. Utilizing secondary entrances only when needed reduces the risk of unauthorized access and the number of personnel needed to man them. To maximize security, guards should be posted at primary entrances unless they are secured or closed. Secondary entrances should remain secure or locked and be patrolled on a regular basis to guard against intrusion.

Entrance, gate, and transportation dock security is especially important in relation to shipping, receiving, and disposal of items. Security controls, including access and egress, are of vital importance in receiving deliveries and making shipments. Gate security should be utilized for directing facility traffic and serving as a means of checking receivables and shipping. Providing an escort of incoming carriers and vendors at the gate until they reach their destination or leave the facility will greatly reduce the opportunity for theft. Guards can also be used to monitor the shipping and receiving departments by comparing shipment invoices with loads, either on a continual or random basis. This is especially important in a facility where expensive goods are produced. These procedures will inhibit drivers and plant employees from falsifying invoices.

The disposal of waste and trash provide opportunities to secret stolen merchandise. Frequently, employees or other persons hide items in trash bins, where they are later retrieved. Periodic checks should be made of trash and disposal areas, and vehicles carrying trash should be randomly checked as they leave the facility. Such precautions will reduce employee thefts and aid in maintaining control over the facility compound. Discarded classified and proprietary information must be destroyed to prevent it from falling into the wrong hands. A new service to enter the security industry is the mobile document-shredding service. Licensed and bonded personnel shred surplus paper documents and provide the client with a certificate of destruction upon completion.

Communication, coordination, and cooperation with management must be maintained to meet the needs of management and security. It is important for the security professional to monitor the facility's operations so adjustments can be made in security as changes in the operations of the facility occur.

People and Hardware

When designing security systems, the security professional has a number of alternative protection devices and personnel at his disposal. It is people and hardware that the professional can utilize to supplement the physical barrier. He must analyze the costs, benefits, and problems associated with each alternative while choosing those that best meet the specific needs of the facility. No single solution is perfect for every job, and the manager must take particular care during this planning stage to analyze his needs.

Perimeter barriers are usually supplemented with guard personnel. Guards serve to boost the deterrent effects of the perimeter barrier and to monitor the barrier for defects. The posting of stationary guards and the use of mobile patrols are largely dependent upon the nature of the facility being guarded and the degree of security needed. When perimeter barriers confine an extremely large area, it may be more efficient to utilize mobile guards to observe the total barrier structure. In isolated or semi-isolated areas, protection may be reduced to infrequent mobile patrols or only an occasional maintenance check. If a high degree of security is desired, it may be necessary to increase patrols or stationary posts, or it may be more cost-effective to construct a second or inner perimeter barrier closer to the area requiring the high-level security."

Although highly reliable as a means of enhancing security, security guards are extremely expensive compared to other physical and electronic security products. The guard force should be reduced to the lowest effective level possible through the use of other security devices such as alarms, clear zones, and high-deterrent barriers.

Other Perimeter Barrier Applications

In many facilities, it is often necessary to construct perimeter barriers around equipment or operations that are especially hazardous or unsafe within an already secured facility. Strict applications may require special compartmentalized security containers. These limited or restricted access areas may be required by the nature of the business conducted or by governmental regulation.

For example, pharmaceutical manufacturers and distributors are required by the Drug Enforcement Agency (DEA) to provide a separate, high-security compartment for controlled substances, narcotics, etc. A good example of a "safety" barrier is a fence surrounding the immediate area of dangerous machinery. Only those people who have both the need and the right level of clearance should be allowed to enter restricted areas.

For safety as well as security reasons, most industrial and manufacturing operations are not open to the general public. The operations and equipment utilized are dangerous to the untrained and unaware non-employee. Perimeter fences serve to deny entry into a hazardous environment. Freedom from interference by outsiders is assured, and organizational liability for improper or inadequate safety measures is avoided. Perimeter barriers are also utilized to complement and supplement fire prevention efforts. Areas containing hazardous materials or processing operations should be separated from the larger facility, allowing for more diligent control of fire regulations and standards. As with security requirements, movable barriers, concertina wire, etc. are particularly useful when temporary conditions exist that are especially hazardous or unsafe.

Chapter Four

Security Lighting

Depending on the nature of the facility, protective lighting may be designed to either emphasize the illumination of the perimeter barrier or the interior of the facility. Lighting can be both functional and ornamental. Effective security programs will ensure that the facility is secure at night as well as during the day. The best method of equalizing security between day and night is the installation of security lighting. Effective lighting enhances the security effort while it serves as a deterrent to criminal activity.

A lighting system must be reliable and designed with overlapping illumination to avoid creating unprotected areas. Design of the exterior security defenses should include lighting in addition to consideration of Duress/Panic Alarm Stations, CCTV, intrusion-detection alarms, and electronic access systems. It is best and most cost-effective to plan for the installation of all exterior electronic protection at one time. Lighting must provide specified levels of illumination:

The Code of Federal Regulations lists a specific requirement of 0.2 foot-candles (fc) for lighting of protected areas within a perimeter.

The National Parking Association recommends illumination of 6 fc at 30 inches above the parking floor within covered parking areas.

The Illinois Engineers Society of North America recommends a minimum of 2 fc illumination in open parking areas.

Safety and security lighting is used to:

- Prevent crime
- Alleviate fear of crime
- Prevent traffic (vehicular and pedestrian) accidents
- Promote social interaction
- Promote business and industry
- Contribute to a positive nighttime visual image
- Provide a pleasing daytime appearance
- Provide inspiration for community spirit and growth
- Provide visual information for vehicular and pedestrian traffic
- Facilitate and direct vehicular and pedestrian traffic flow

Lighting Terminology

When planning lighting systems, it is important to be familiar with the terminology used in rating the effectiveness of various lamps. Commonly used terms include:

Candlepower – One candlepower is the amount of light emitted by one standard candle. This standard has been established by the National Bureau of Standards and is commonly used to rate various systems.

Foot-candle – One foot-candle equals one lumen of light per square foot of space. The density or intensity of illumination is measured in foot-candles. The more intense the light, the higher the foot-candle rating for the light.

Lumen – One lumen is the amount of light required to light an area of one square foot to one candlepower. Most lamps are rated in lumens.

Brightness – Brightness refers to the ratio of illumination to that which is being observed. High brightness on certain backgrounds causes glare, and low brightness levels on some backgrounds make observation difficult. Brightness, therefore, should not be too low or too high relative to the field of vision.

Types of Security Lighting

Security lighting is divided into four general categories:

- Continuous lighting
- Standby lighting
- Movable lighting
- Emergency lighting

The type of lighting selected will depend upon the nature of the security application.

Continuous, or stationary, lighting is the most common type of protective lighting. Continuous lighting is the installation of a series of fixed luminaries so that a particular area is flooded with overlapping cones of light.

Standby lighting configurations are similar to continuous lighting except that standby lights are not continuously lit, but are manually or automatically turned on in specific, predetermined situations. The lighting may be activated manually or by a number of automatic means, such as timing devices, intrusion detectors, etc.

Movable lighting systems are manually operated and mobile. Movable lighting should be available to supplement continuous or standby lighting. Additionally, movable lighting should be available to enhance security operations where security is not normally provided, for example, during an operation at an infrequently used loading dock.

Emergency lighting is a system that, by its nature, attempts to duplicate all of the above systems. It is generally used in situations where regular lighting is inoperable during power outages or emergencies. Such a system must include its own power source, generators, etc.

Types of Lighting

Incandescent or filament lamps are common glass light bulbs. These bulbs are commonly used in homes and the work place. Their use is somewhat limited in security systems because of their low rated life and their lower lumens per electrical watt rating.

Mercury vapor lamps are more efficient than incandescent lamps. They emit a bluish cast and are used to light both interior and exterior work areas. They are more efficient than incandescent because of their considerably longer lamp life and can withstand reductions in electrical power of up to 50 percent.

Sodium vapor lamps are similar in construction to the mercury vapor lamps, and are the most efficient lamps in use today. They are widely used in areas where fog is a frequent problem and are frequently found on highways and bridges. High-pressure sodium lamps produce up to 140 lumens of light per watt and have a rated life of 15,000 hours. Sodium vapor lamps provide excellent security lighting, especially around perimeter barriers, because of their efficiency. Today, many streets in high crime areas use sodium vapor lamps.

Fluorescent lamps have a rated life of up to 14,000 hours, but they do not produce as much light as some of the other lamps. They are usually found in work areas since the light is not as distracting as some of the gaseous discharge lamps.

The selection of a light source is dependent upon a number of considerations:

- Cleaning and replacement of lamps and luminaries, particularly with respect to the costs and means (e.g., ladders, mechanical "brackets," etc.) required and available
- The advisability of including manual and remote controls and mercury of photoelectric controls
- The effects of local weather conditions on various types of lamps and luminaries
- Fluctuating or erratic voltages in the primary power source
- The requirement for grounding of fixtures and the use of a common ground on an entire line to provide a stable ground potential

Types of Lighting Equipment

There are four basic types of lighting equipment available:

- Flood lights
- Streetlights
- Fresnel units
- Search lights

The usage of a particular type is dependent upon the security requirement.

Floodlights project light in a concentrated area. They are used to light a particular point or area. Floodlights are manufactured with a variety of beam widths, allowing the appropriate light to meet the needs of the task. Because floodlights emit a directed beam, they work well in instances that call for glare projection lighting, i.e., the illumination of boundaries, buildings, or fences.

Streetlights emit diffused light rather than a directional beam. They generally produce little glare and are appropriate for use in controlled lighting situations. They are commonly used to light parking lots, thoroughfares, facility entrances, and boundary perimeters where glare is detrimental. Because of their efficiency, streetlights can be deployed to light large areas at a minimum cost.

Fresnel units emit a fan-shaped beam of light, illuminating a field of approximately 180 degrees horizontally and 15 to 30 degrees vertically. Fresnel units are the most effective units when glare lighting is desired because of their projection pattern. Fresnel units are employed to illuminate areas between buildings and perimeters.

Searchlights produce a highly focused, intense beam of light. They can be directed to any location inside or outside the property, and although they can be automated, most are manually operated and are often used to complement existing lighting systems.

Designing a Lighting System

Selection of a lighting system and fixtures is dependent upon the use of the system and the needs of the environment. When a perimeter fence is at least one hundred feet from structures or work areas and there is a clear zone on the outside of the perimeter, then either controlled illumination or glare projection techniques are adequate. Both techniques would adequately illuminate the barrier. When guards or patrol units are used, they should be posted outside the illuminated areas. Lighting should be deployed to provide full illumination of the barrier, but must not interfere with guard activities, traffic (both on and offsite), or other businesses or activities inside or outside the perimeter.

Lighting systems should be installed in a manner that affords the greatest possible illumination of the facility being protected without negatively affecting the vision of people engaged in work, driving, walking, etc. Entrances for pedestrian and vehicular traffic should be lit using controlled lighting. The lighting should be intense enough to enable guards to recognize persons and to examine credentials and other papers.

If the entry point has a gatehouse, the level of illumination should be lower so that those approaching will have difficulty observing the activities of the guard. Work areas within the compound, especially those where materials and merchandise are being loaded and unloaded, should be illuminated with some form of continuous lighting to provide for safety and security.

There are three major factors to consider in planning the security lighting system: security needs, costs, and operations safety. Each safety and security situation must be thoroughly examined with these factors in mind. Only after a complete analysis is made can the best lighting configuration be devised and deployed.

Planning

Frequently, lighting serves to advertise a product or service during the evening hours. This can cause problems, however, for the security manager when aesthetic qualities take precedence over safety and security concerns. The security professional would probably prefer flood lamps mounted near the roof, out of the reach of potential intruders, and directed downward, exposing a large area immediately adjacent to the structure. Conversely, the owner may prefer floodlights mounted on the ground, illuminating the exterior of the building or a sign for advertising purposes. When protective lighting is used for advertising purposes, it frequently compromises security efforts.

Protective lighting is used to facilitate pedestrian and vehicular traffic within a compound. Roads, entrances, exits, pathways, and parking facilities should be illuminated during darkness. A conflict may arise when the same lighting is used to promote safety and security. Spotlights from above for example, may interfere with the operation of a motor vehicle.

Finally, security lighting is deployed to deter unauthorized access and egress from a facility, and when it does not deter, it aids in the subsequent detection and apprehension of intruders. The commission of a crime includes three elements: the desire, the ability, and the opportunity. Effectively deployed, security lighting can reduce or eliminate all three.

The placement of security lighting depends on each specific location, structure, and requirement. The type of perimeter being protected, its location, and activities determine the protective lighting system needed. For example, a facility adjacent to a public highway should not use glare lighting.

In planning for an effective security lighting layout, there are four visual factors that must be taken into consideration: size, brightness, contrast, and time. The lighting layout depends on the desired degree of security and the nature of the objects and environment being secured.

Generally, larger objects require less light than smaller objects. The larger the object, the more light it will reflect, thus requiring less illumination. Brightness refers to the reflective ability of the object or structure. Light colors, such as white, reflect more light than dark colors, such as black or brown. Thus, a building painted white would require less light than comparable buildings constructed of dark brick.

Additionally, the texture of the objects under observation affects needed light intensity. Coarsely textured objects tend to diffuse light, whereas smooth surfaced objects tend to reflect light, reducing the need for higher-intensity protective lighting. Contrast refers to the relative shapes and colors of objects under observation in relation to the total environment. If there is contrast between the objects being secured and the immediate environment, observation is much easier than if there was little relative contrast.

Finally, time refers to the fact that greater illumination is required for areas that are visually complex or crowded, because this makes it harder to scan quickly or for extended periods. Open spaces, on the other hand, require less light because the observer has more time to observe and focus on seemingly foreign objects. When planning security lighting patterns, it is important to consider all four of these visual factors.

During the planning stages, the following data should be collected: Descriptions, characteristics, and specifications of the various incandescent, arc, and gaseous discharge lamps, the lighting patterns of the various units, typical layouts showing the most efficient placement, height and spacing of equipment, and the minimum protective lighting intensities required for various applications.

Chapter Five

Locks

The physical security of any property or facility starts with its locking system. Locking devices vary greatly in appearance, function, and application. Regardless of their type, locks are primarily delaying devices. The degree of delay is dependent upon its quality of construction and installation and the skill of the would-be intruder. The locking device is usually the first line of defense, whether it is on a perimeter fence, a door to the facility, or an interior office.

Locks

Locks date back some three thousand years. Locks provide varying degrees and manners of security. Properly employed, locks will discourage burglars, thieves, or other would-be criminals. To serve as more than delaying devises, locks should be utilized in conjunction with other security hardware as part of the overall security envelope.

Single-Cylinder Locking Devices

These locking devices are installed in doors or placed on other objects that must be secured from only one side. They require a key to open them from one side. The most likely application of a single-cylinder locking device would be on a solid door far enough from glass panels or windows so that an intruder cannot break the glass, reach in, and open the door from the other side. Most locking devices of this type have a thumb turn on the inside of the door. This permits easy locking or unlocking of the door, which is sometimes important for reasons of safety or quick exit.

Double-Cylinder Locking Devices

This type of locking device is installed on doors that must be secured from both sides. A key is required to open or lock the door from either side. A door with glass panels or one next to glass panels would likely be fitted with a double-cylinder locking device. Such locking devices may not be feasible for use in schools, hospitals, fire exits, etc., where for reasons of safety their use would be prohibited.

Emergency Exit Locking Devices

These devices allow for quick exit without use of a key, usually by means of a horizontal "panic bar." The device locks the door against entry, and in many instances, no external hardware is apparent at all. Frequently, these emergency exits have an audible alarm device that sounds when the exit is used or an electronic alarm as part of an electronic access system.

Electromagnetic Locking Devices

Electromagnetic locking devices respond to an electric current, which creates an electromagnetic action that releases the strike. These locks are utilized more for remote operation and convenience than for high levels of security.

Recording Devices

While not a locking device itself, an electronic access system installed in conjunction with locks will provide a record of door use by time of day or by key used.

Vertical-Throw Locking Devices

Several variations are available in vertical-throw locking devices. While a vertical-throw bolt can be found in a rim lock, single-cylinder lock, double-cylinder lock, etc., there are variations that do not require a key and can only be opened or locked from the secured side of the door. An example of this is the "police lock," which uses an angled bar that fits into a receptacle in the floor and is secured to the door at the other end. Another variation is the vertical bolt, which can be installed in the floor or on the bottom of the door in a recessed position, and is pushed down into a floor well to prevent the door from opening.

Sequence Locking Device

Sequence locking devices are used to ensure that doors are closed and locked in a predetermined order. Each door is locked in its sequence, and no door can be locked until its designated predecessor has been locked. This locking system prevents the forgotten unlocked door.

Keying Systems

A key is the standard method of locking and unlocking doors. Most key-operated locks are manufactured to accept a unique key that has been specifically designed and cut to fit it. Locks of any function, quality, or effectiveness are worthless if keys are not available to those who need them or are not themselves secure and accounted for. Keys and keying systems are generally divided into change keys, maison keys, control keys, sub-master keys, master keys, and grand master keys.

The change key fits a single lock within a master key system or any other single lock unnumbered by such a system. Numerous locks can be "keyed alike" to accept only one key. For example, entry locksets sold in hardware and department stores for residential applications may have four or five different key patterns among an entire batch of sets for sale. This is convenient for the homeowner buying three or four lock sets for his home, as only one key will be required. However, there can be many locksets sold from the same store with the same key pattern.

The maison key is a sub-master key system common in apartment houses and office buildings. Tenants are provided with a single key that operates both their apartment or office door and the main entrance door lock. This is an insecure system of keying and should be utilized only in conjunction with other security measures.

Master Key Systems

The process of master keying consists of splitting the bottom pin into two or more segments so that keys of different combinations (cuts) will raise bottom pins and master pins to a shear line. As the number of locks in a master key system increases and as the progressive stages of master keying increase, so does the number of master pins and shear lines. With each increase, there is a resulting decrease in security because the chances of arriving at or finding a shear line for each pin by picking is increased sharply. There can be progressive stages of master keying. The following keys are found in a simple master key system.

Sub-master – This is a key that will open all locks of a particular area, zone, or region within a given application.

Master key – The master key will open all the locks in an application that are part of the master key system.

Grand master key – This key will open every lock in a keying system involving two or more master key groups.

Control key – A control key is used for maintenance or replacement purposes. It is designed in such a way that it removes the core from the housing, allowing for a rapid and cost-effective method to replace or exchange cores. It is recommended to change locks or cores to prevent or rectify key inventory problems.

Key Control

A system must be established and enforced that accounts for and controls every key and every lock. Responsibility and authority must be given to someone (preferably, the security department) to maintain records, provide for a key depository, control issuance and retrieval, and investigate any misuse or loss of facility keys and locks. Keys, especially masters and sub-masters, should be stamped "DO NOT DUPLICATE." When conducting the security survey, it is likely that you will discover discrepancies with regards to the key inventory and control.

A written log should be maintained on all keys and locks. The issuance of keys should be controlled to only those persons who have been shown to have a need for keys. When a key is issued, the record should indicate the key number, the name of the person to whom it is assigned, his position within the company, the date of issuance, and any other relevant data. The key log should include records of maintenance and repairs on locks, lost keys, and actions taken to remedy any problems detrimental to lock and key security. All keys should be identified and secured in a high-security key cabinet.

Key Depository

Although often not feasible or appropriate, it would be best if no keys to the facility ever left the premises, the closer this goal can be approached, the greater the degree of security a facility has over controlling access to its property. Keys removed from the property can be duplicated, lost, or used in some other way to compromise facility security. The ideal method for high-security applications would be for all employees who were issued keys each day to turn in or deposit the keys with security personnel at quitting time. A log of daily issuance and return would ensure that all keys were properly issued and accounted for.

Master Key Control

Master keys must be treated with greater care and security than change keys. The loss of a master key threatens the entire keying system. The first rule of key control is to minimize the number of keys issued, particularly master keys. Keys must not be issued for convenience, nor should they be issued on the basis of an employee's position. They should be issued on a basis of need. The indiscriminate issuing of keys is little improvement over having no locks at all.

Master and sub-master keys should not be marked or inscribed in any way that would identify them as master keys. An internal coding identification system should be developed that is known only by necessary personnel. Whenever a key is issued, a lock becomes more vulnerable to being compromised through the theft, loss, improper use, or duplication of the key. The loss or theft of a master key can result in a sizeable cost to re-key and the possible loss of property.

Combination Locks

Commonly found on safes, vaults, high-security storage containers, and high-security padlocks, the dial-type combination locks do not require keys to operate the lock mechanism. The combination-locking device, provided it is of good quality and installed properly, affords a greater degree of security than most key-operated locking devices. The integrity and security of a combination lock can be more effectively maintained than a key-operated lock.

The combination must be considered strictly confidential and be restricted to an absolute minimum of personnel. Any written record of the combination must be afforded the highest security and, if feasible, no such record should even be kept. As in re-coring cylinder locks, combinations should be changed periodically as a matter of procedure and changed after the termination or transfer of any employee who knows the combination or worked in close proximity to the storage unit. Changes should be made any time there is an indication that the security of the combination has been compromised.

Padlocks

Perhaps the most familiar locks, padlocks have a variety of security applications: gates, doors, storage areas, equipment lockouts, employee lockers, chains, and tool chests. They can be incorporated into a master key system or be operated by a change key. A key-operated padlock has three basic parts: the key, the casing, and the shackle. The casing houses the internal locking mechanism and the core (keyway). The shackle is the locking, or holding, part of the padlock.

A padlock is only effective when the surface on which it is installed is of solid construction. The hasp should be casehardened, installed properly, and not expose the mounting screws or bolts when in the locked position. Security guards or facilities maintenance personnel should routinely inspect such padlocks and the attached fastening devices for evidence of compromise or deterioration.

Other lock types include:

- Pin tumbler
- Deadbolt
- Spring-loaded latch
- Warded
- Disc tumbler
- Lever locks

Locks, like other security hardware, vary in quality and application. The professional security consultant should become familiar with the various lock types and remain vigilant for violations of key inventories and proper maintenance. A professional licensed and bonded locksmith should be part of the security professional's network.

Attacks Against Locks

Direct forcible assault is the most common course of unauthorized access. More highly skilled criminals may direct their attempts at access against locks. The most common method of gaining entry through a locked door or other fixture is to use a key. Persons using lost or misappropriated keys can accomplish unauthorized access with the use of a key. The professional thief may have a selection of "masters" or lock-picking equipment at his disposal. Surreptitious violations and physical assaults include cutting, picking, jimmying, prying, jacking, smashing, carding, and drilling.

Picking is a method by which the lock's tumblers are manipulated through the keyhole using small tools made for this purpose. Picking a cylinder is usually done in one of two ways. One method is using a small tool called a tension wrench, which puts tension on the plug and hence on the pins that are impeding the rotation of the plug. With this tension tightening the pins, the pick is inserted to raise the pins, one by one, to the right level until the shear line is obtained for all the pins. Another method is "raking," where a thin metal tool is inserted into and then quickly pulled out of the keyway, jostling the pins into position.

Carding, or "loiding," is the action of slipping or shimming a spring bolt using a piece of celluloid (driver's license, etc.). A spring-loaded latch that does not resist end pressure is particularly susceptible to carding.

Jacking is the act of placing a car jack or hydraulic jacking devise horizontally between the doorjambs and applying pressure. A poorly constructed door or one not sufficiently fortified will spread, pulling the bolt or latch out of the strike and allowing the door to open.

Crowbars, smaller jimmy bars, large screwdrivers, or other metal tools are used to jimmy, or pry, the door away from its frame or break the locking mechanism. Vertical-locking devices will usually offer greater resistance to jimmying than horizontal devices.

Smashing is the simple physical assault on a door. Smashing ranges from total destruction of the door to the breaking of a glass panel to gain access to a thumb turn. Assorted tools can be used to smash a door. This method occurs when a building or other structure is located in an area remote enough that the noise created by the smashing is not a deterrent to breaking in.

Removing hinge pins is another method used to defeat locking systems. Hinges should be located on the interior side of the door, but if they are exposed, they should be welded in position or otherwise made non-removable.

Basic Door Locks

Crime statistics indicate that half of all illegal entries occur through a door. Accordingly, doors and windows should be designed and installed to protect against surreptitious violations and physical assaults. Windows are the point of entry in about forty percent of illegal entries.

Windows and doors are chosen as points of entry because they are the most common openings in buildings. Someone attempting illegal entry into a building or facility usually bases his choice on the perceived ease of entry and the level of risk involved. The ease of entry has a direct relationship to the level of risk taking – the easier the entry, the lower the risk. Some locks are more secure than others and present a more formidable barrier to surreptitious entry.

The Key-in-the-Knob

One of the most frequently used door locks today is the key-in-the-knob. This lock, like the one on the bathroom door in your home, is almost always the least secure type of available door lock. The typical key-in-the-knob lock is too susceptible to failure or breakage to be considered a security lock.

Auxiliary Locks

Auxiliary locks are added to a door or other opening to supplement the existing locking device. Adding an auxiliary lock is usually the simplest and most cost-effective way to bolster the security offered by the present, primary door lock. Two types of auxiliary locks are used most often.

A rim lock with a vertical- or horizontal-bolt throw is a common auxiliary lock. When properly installed, a rim lock of the single cylinder or double cylinder variety with a deadbolt provides a substantial level of security. It is resistant to jimmying, prying, carding and jacking.

The deadbolt tubular lock, either single- or double-cylinder variety, can be added with minimum difficulty and affords an improved degree of security over many primary lock types.

The Mortise Lock

To install a mortise lock, a cavity (mortise) must be cut in the door to receive the lock. The bolt is made so that a hole must be cut in the edge of the door. Mortise locks provide an acceptable level of security because most of the lock mechanism is in a metal enclosure within the door. Mortise locks are available in single- or double-cylinder varieties and may have additional functions, such as an automatic-locking capability from one or both sides of the door.

Window Locks

Most windows, when installed, are provided with a latch, but these offer little protection. There are a number of specialty locks available for windows. There are also both keyed and non-keyed devices that provide a greater level of protection than the latch. Window devices are particularly important in ground floor applications or on windows near accessible stairs, fire escapes, etc.

The sliding glass door serves as both a window and a door. Manufacturer-supplied locking mechanisms usually do not afford a high level of security. There is a variety of locking devices available that will increase protection to acceptable levels. These devises are designed to make it more difficult to raise, slide, or force the unit open.

Chapter Six

Electronic Alarm and Access Systems

NOTE: Electronic security technology is ever-changing and evolving. The professional security consultant must keep abreast of these changes. Alarm companies, manufacturers, and vendors provide training and demonstrations of their latest products and peripheral equipment.

Electronic protection of people and property continues to receive great attention. Electronics are utilized to provide perimeter security of buildings, doors and windows, access control, control of interior movements, environmental controls, and to detect fire problems. Technology is advancing so rapidly in the area of electronic intrusion detection systems that more and more areas of property are being included. Parking lots, outdoor storage facilities, interior offices, cabinets and safes, and personnel are some areas that are now protected by electronics.

As seen elsewhere in this book, physical security is a matter of degree. With adequate time, equipment, and skills, an intruder can penetrate virtually any facility. Intrusion systems must be evaluated in terms of cost effectiveness. A balance of electronic security features, security personnel, and public law enforcement services should be achieved to provide adequate levels of protection. Over dependence in one component of the system can increase costs beyond benefits, whereas under dependence may result in the degradation of the security system.

To be considered effective, all components of a security system must satisfy two practical tests: (1) The system must function the way it was designed and (2) It must be cost-effective for the application. Systems that fail either of these tests should be redesigned.

Alarm Systems

The functions of the alarm system are: (1) Detect fire, intrusion, and environmental concerns (2) Make emergency notifications and (3) Monitor building and equipment functions and conditions. Properly designed systems can incorporate all of the above. Systems can also be designed to place emphasis on the priorities of the application, i.e., one facility may have a greater need for intrusion detection than environmental control. Alarm systems should be designed and installed with the specific needs of the client in mind. The four basic types of alarms are defined by their points of termination:

- Central-station alarm systems
- Local alarm systems
- Proprietary central-control alarm systems
- Auxiliary alarm systems

The needs of the client usually dictate which of the four basic types of signal termination are most effective and appropriate.

Central-Station Alarms

Central-station alarm systems monitor fire, intrusion (burglary) environmental, and other conditions through the activation of a receiving module over telephone lines at a location separate from the facility being protected by the system.

Central-station alarm companies are frequently privately owned businesses. They employ trained personnel who generally monitor several alarm systems from a central location twenty-four hours per day, seven days per week.

When an alarm activates a sensor, the person monitoring the alarm signal will either notify the fire or police department, dispatch a security officer, contact designated facility personnel, or any combination of those things, as set up in the standard operating procedures. An activated fire sensor requires that the fire department be notified. If the activated sensor is an intrusion alarm, security personnel should be dispatched to the facility and follow their standing operational procedures. Generally, they should await the arrival of police before entering the facility.

Local Alarms

Local alarm notification systems terminate on-site at either a central control station or in the vicinity of the activated sensor. Local alarms can be visual, audible, or both. Local alarm systems are only effective when someone is present at the facility at all times to monitor the alarms. Without security or monitoring personnel present, local alarm systems do not afford adequate levels of protection. Because they are usually simple in design, unmanned local alarm systems are usually easily defeated, their audible alarms go unanswered and provide little deterrence, and they frequently sound false alarms.

When a company uses outside audible alarms, plans for appropriate response to the alarm by a representative of the facility must be made. If a response plan is not in effect, local alarm systems should be set on a timer so that the alarm will automatically shut off after a predetermined time. Many jurisdictions have strict regulations on the time limits brought on by frequent unwarranted or nuisance alarms.

Proprietary Central-Control Alarms

Proprietary central-control alarm systems are privately owned and controlled and are similar to central station systems. a central-control system, alarms are monitored by a central station within the facility and not at a distant location. These stations are usually staffed twenty-four hours a day, seven days a week, and the response to alarms is made by dispatching designated personnel to the alarm. These proprietary systems serve only one owner but may protect multiple facilities. By design, response time by a proprietary security force to an alarm from a proprietary central-control alarm is considerably faster than with a central station alarm system. Proprietary systems almost always cost more to operate than the contracted services of a central station alarm system.

Auxiliary Alarm Systems

Auxiliary alarm systems involve notification directly to a police department, fire department, or other telephone number, and are usually silent alarm systems. Direct notification systems require either line or radio communications between the alarm system and the notification point, the most frequent being a telephone line leased for that specific purpose. The methods of contact include the programmed tape dialers, the digital dialers, and the direct connectors.

Tape Dialer – Tape dialers call a programmed telephone number when the alarm system is activated. When the telephone is answered, a recording sends the receiver a coded message describing the alarm condition. The message repeats until contact is made. This system is easily defeated, however, by interrupting the telephone circuit, thus breaking the telephonic contact. Also, the tape used for delivering any recorded phone numbers and messages usually sit idle for long periods of time, allowing the tape to dry out and become brittle. Activation after such durations usually causes the tape to break, resulting in no notification at all. Tape dialer technology is obsolete and, if implemented, should be used as a back-up system only and tested regularly.

Digital Dialer – Rather than sending programmed messages, digital dialers transmit a coded message to a special receiver that can be located at the police department, fire department, or other location. The coded message, usually numerical, indicates the nature and location of the alarm so that an appropriate response can be made.

Direct Connect – Direct connect alarm systems use an exclusive, designated telephone transmission circuit called a "dry line" that connects the alarm system directly to a specific location. Alarms are received by modular alarm units, which detect activity generated by circuit malfunctions or alarm activation. Direct connect systems are limited by their ability to transmit only three individual conditions: an "all clear" signal, meaning no activity or alarm; a generic "trouble" condition, showing some system violation or phone line failure; and a nonspecific "alarm" signal. These limitations reduce the desirability of this system as a first line of defense.

Although still quite common, auxiliary alarm systems have created problems for public services such as police and fire protection. Many jurisdictions have placed strict limitations on the number and types of organizations that can have direct contact systems linked to their emergency service departments.

Fundamentals of Alarm Systems

Alarm systems are composed of five basic components:

- Devices and sensors that monitor and react to a change in the environment
- A control unit that acts as a signal-processing unit
- An enunciator, either silent or local, that generates human response.
- A power supply from a commercial power source or alternative battery power source
- Circuitry, either hard wire or wireless, for transmission of signals

These five basic components are common to most alarm systems regardless of their function or purpose. Whether an alarm system is designed for detection of fire, detection of intrusion, emergency notification, or monitoring of equipment or facility conditions, the operating principles of each are much the same.

Control Unit

The control unit is the terminating point for all sensors and switches in the alarm system. It can be designed to have a variety of capabilities, from a simple on-off switch to an integrated system of sensors and switches divided into zones and functions. Control units are usually housed in heavy, steel, tamper-resistant containers.

Elements of the control unit are arranged to receive signals from the sensors and to relay signals to the appropriate termination point. System control is usually accomplished through an integrated keypad or command station that allows authorized personnel the ability to turn the system on or off, bypass problem or faulted areas, and perform various system diagnostics.

Enunciator

The enunciator is a visual or audible signaling device that detects and indicates activation of the alarm system. Selection of the appropriate annunciation for an alarm system depends upon two factors: (1) the circumstances and location surrounding the alarm system site, and (2) the desired or required orientation of the alarm system. Often, the location of a facility or the availability of alarm services mandate that either a local alarm or remote, silent alarm be employed.

When choosing the type of annunciation, particularly with an intrusion detection system, one must make the choice between an apprehension-oriented system (the silent alarm) and the deterrent-oriented system (the local alarm).

Power Source

The primary power source for alarm systems is obtained from commercial power sources. The input voltage is reduced and rectified to provide a direct current (DC) of the proper voltage to the system. In the event that the commercial power is disrupted, a back up means of energy, usually a "battery back-up," is required to provide a continuous, uninterrupted source of electrical power.

Alarm Circuits

The alarm circuit transmits signals from the sensors to the control unit, which in turn transmits signals to the local or remote enunciator-receiving unit. Alarm systems are wired as either "open" or "closed" circuits. The open circuit system is a line without a flow of current present until a switch or relay is closed, completing the circuit. The closed circuit system is a line with current flowing through it, and any change in this flow will initiate an alarm signal.

Selection of Alarm Systems

The following elements should be considered during design and prior to installation:

- Importance of the facility, materials, and processes.
- Vulnerability of the facility, materials, and processes.
- Appropriateness and feasibility of using specific types of alarm systems.
- Initial and recurring costs of the alarm system compared to the cost (in money or security) of possible loss of materials or information.
- Savings in manpower and money over a period of time.
- Response time by security personnel or other respondents.
- Improvement over current security methods.
- Decisions to utilize electronic alarm systems should lead to economy and improvement over existing security practices and methods.

Alarm Devices and Sensors

Alarm devices and equipment are usually classified into three general categories, according to the type of physical protection coverage provided:

- Point, or spot, protection;
- Area, or space, protection; and
- Perimeter protection.

An electronic security system can provide the desired type and depth of protection by combining two or more of these categories.

Intrusion Detection Alarm Devices and Sensors (Burglar Alarms)

Intrusion detection alarm systems serve to detect and deter unauthorized entry and exit of a facility, building, or other structure. Requirements at a specific site to be protected determine which devices or equipment are most effective and appropriate. Some common devices and their characteristics are:

Electromechanical Devices (Perimeter-Point)

The most commonly used alarm sensors are electro-mechanical—sensors that activate by breaking or closing an electrical circuit. Electromechanical systems function in a way that requires a current-carrying conductor (wire) and an intrusion detector to be placed in a position between a potential intruder and the place being protected.

Switches are commonly utilized in electromechanical alarm systems. The most common type is the magnetic contact switch. The standard magnetic switch consists of a switch unit and a magnet. The magnet is usually attached to a movable fixture and the "switch" unit to a permanent fixture. When moved, the magnetic portion of the unit causes the switch component to either make or break the electrical circuit connection, thus sending the alarm.

Another common electromechanical device is metallic window foil applied to the glass in windows and doors. The foil tape is cemented on the glass and forms a complete circuit and, if broken, will activate the alarm system. A basic advantage afforded by window foil is the psychological deterrence it has on would-be intruders, as it is obvious to outsiders that an alarm system is present. The problem with window foil, however, is the installation and maintenance associated with it is quite labor-intensive.

Windows with insect screening can be protected by a method called "alarm screening." The original screening material is removed and replaced with a new type fabric that has fine insulated wires woven into it connected to the protective loop in such a way that cutting the screen or removing it, frame and all, will activate the alarm.

Electromechanical devices are used primarily to provide perimeter protection for buildings or other structures. Individually, the devices provide point-protection of a window, door, or other opening, but taken together, they create a perimeter line of alarm protection.

Advantages of electromechanical sensor devices are:

- Once installed, they usually provide relatively maintenance-free service. Environmental conditions will affect switches and metallic window foil on exterior units.
- Not being sophisticated systems allows them to operate without excessive numbers of nuisance alarms.
- They provide good perimeter security in low risk situations.

Disadvantages of electromechanical sensor devices are:

- The system can be easily compromised; walls and roof are not usually covered.
- It can be costly to install in a facility with many coverage points, there is a lack of local standards on installation and maintenance of various systems, and they will not detect persons who remain in the building without permission.

Photoelectric Devices (Space-Point-Perimeter)

The photoelectric type of intrusion detection device uses a light-sensitive cell and a projected light source. The light beam is projected from a transmitter unit to a receiving unit (photoelectric cell.) When an intruder interrupts the beam, the contact with the photoelectric cell is broken and the alarm is activated. The transmitter and receiver can be arranged in such a way that mirrored reflectors can be used to obtain a crisscrossed pattern of coverage. The light source can be white, infrared, or laser. The most common one in use is the infrared because of its invisibility and ease of purchase. Coverage from infrared units can include point, perimeter, or area, depending upon their arrangement.

Advantages of photoelectric detectors are:

Useful at entrances, exits, and driveways where obstructive devices cannot be used, when properly installed and used, can provide reliable security, and may be used to activate other security or safety devices, i.e., cameras and fire extinguishers.

Disadvantages of photoelectric detectors are:

When used outdoors, rain, fog, dust, and smoke can interfere with the light beam, they must be used in locations where it will not be possible to go over or under the light beam, and they require frequent maintenance inspections of units and the grounds.

Audio/Acoustic Devices (Space or Point)

Sensitive microphones are installed in the protected area and are adjusted to tolerate the ambient sound levels in the environment. Attempts to gain forced entry into the area generate "abnormal" sounds and noises that activate the alarm. Acoustic devices are usually tuned to detect the frequency of breaking glass. Most acoustic detectors usually require a vibration signal in combination with the proper glass-breaking frequency in order to generate an alarm. These sensors can be used to cover large areas of glass. Audio devices can be used as audio monitors that provide a capability of "listening in" on the environment being protected. Microphones in the audio detectors can be linked to a voice-grade telephone line connected to a specially equipped central station. An operator can then monitor the situation to determine if an actual emergency exists.

Motion Detectors (Space)

There are two primary types of enclosed space motion detectors: infrared and microwave.

Microwave motion detectors generate high-frequency radio waves, filling a specific enclosed area with a pattern of radio waves. Motion within the prescribed area will interfere with, and change the frequency of, the radio waves, thus activating the alarm.

Infrared motion detectors employ passive infrared heat-seeking technology that detects intruders by detecting slight variations in temperature caused by the intruder's body (which is infrared energy). Unlike the photoelectric type of intrusion detector, the passive infrared motion detector does not emit infrared energy, but only detects it.

The most stable and efficient type of motion detector is a combination unit consisting of both microwave and infrared technologies. Combination units require movement (microwave) and body heat (infrared) to be detected before triggering an alarm.

Pressure-Sensitive Devices (Point)

Pressure-sensitive devices are usually placed in a location where an intruder is likely to walk. Pressure-sensitive, or stress-sensitive, devices are used to detect changes or shifts in weight and can be utilized as alarms or a "type of doorbell" to announce arrivals and departures of people. Contact stress detectors can be placed under stairways or on floor joists to detect weight or stress changes. Pressure devices are also applicable to placement under art objects, store merchandise, etc., to detect movement.

Capacity Devices (Point)

The electromagnetic, or capacitance, type device can be installed on metallic objects such as metal fences, safes, and filing cabinets. With this device, the protected metal object itself becomes part of the system and serves as the capacitance of a tuned circuit. When changes occur within the proximity of the protected object, such as the approach of a person, there is a sufficient change in the capacitance to upset the balance of the system and cause an alarm. Unlike space alarms, the protective field around the protected object can be adjusted down to a depth of a few inches from its surface. In this way, objects can be protected day or night, even during business hours. Capacity devices have a high degree of security but are restricted in application because they can only be applied to ungrounded metal objects.

Fire Detection Systems

Fire is one of the most destructive and feared forces known to man. Man-made or natural, potential loss of life and property by fire can be devastating. Accordingly, protection of life and property from fire is of utmost importance in the safety and security program of any business or facility. Measures must be taken to prevent the occurrence of and to detect and suppress fire.

Alarm systems and devices designed to detect fire can either be incorporated into or parallel intrusion alarm systems. However, many jurisdictions have requirements for fire systems that are far more stringent than for security systems. Often, these jurisdictions regulate fire safety through the fire department or other agency and have strict rules and regulations regarding the operation of fire systems. These rules and regulations can vary greatly across the country. Security consultants must check with the appropriate authorities as part of a comprehensive survey or consult to ensure accuracy in compliance.

Fire detection and alarm systems serve to notify the appropriate responders of an emergency. These systems should also include local alarms in conjunction with a central station, proprietary central station, or auxiliary system. Fire systems are designed to provide the earliest possible alarm in the case of fire to protect people and property.

Fire Detection Devices

There are two general types of heat-sensing devices:

- Fixed Temperature – These operate at a predetermined temperature.
- Rate-of-Rise – These respond to unusual variations or increases in temperature.

Fixed-temperature detectors are used extensively in protective signaling systems. This device employs the principle of different coefficients of expansion in metals (bimetallic strip or disc), similar to a common thermostat. Heat causes the expansion of the two ("bi") metal products, which expand at different rates. The difference in expansion rates causes the heated metal to move or bend. The subsequent movement of the electrical contacts closes an electrical circuit and activates the alarm. Other types depend upon heat melting a heat-sensitive plastic or other type of insulation.

Rate-of-rise detectors (thermocouple devices) react to sudden, rapid changes in temperature and can be set to operate more quickly than fixed-temperature detectors.

Smoke Detectors

In many fire situations, detection is enhanced by the addition or inclusion of smoke detectors in the fire alarm system. Most commercial applications of smoke detectors are the photoelectric and ionization devices. Photoelectric smoke detectors are activated by smoke interrupting a photoelectric beam. Ionization smoke detectors react to the hydrocarbons that develop during the chemical processes of the pre-ignition stages of fire.

The security consultant may also encounter other smoke and fire detection devises, including rate-compensated detectors, laser beam fire detectors, and ultraviolet or infrared flame detectors.

Emergency Notification Systems

Emergency notification systems are used to provide warnings during unusual or dangerous situations. Panic or duress alarms and bank robbery notification alarms are perhaps the most common examples of the emergency notification system. These systems can be designed to provide both local and off-site notification. Strategic placement of devices within a facility can alert the police or others of an emergency in progress. Robbery alarms should be silent and activated only when safe to do so.

Local audible and visual alarms can be used to notify employees of an actual or imminent emergency within a facility or work area. When used as part of a comprehensive emergency action plan, whistles, bells, sirens, lights, and similar devices are effective in warning people to take cover, evacuate, or take some other (planned) action. These systems and devices can be used to warn of fires, explosions, or other man-made or natural disasters.

False Alarms

False alarms are a problem—a big problem. Alarm systems are effective in detecting and deterring burglars, but they are subject to certain inherent problems, the most problematic being the false alarm. Some estimates report that 90 to 98 percent of all alarms transmitted are false. These false alarms are usually attributed to one of the following factors: (1) user error or negligence (lack of training); (2) poor installation, maintenance, or service; and (3) faulty equipment.

User error or negligence is responsible for over 50 percent of all false alarms. The security consultant should examine client records to determine what that client's alarm rates are. If unsatisfactory rates of alarms or false alarms are found, the consultant should assist the client in establishing a training program. Frequently, especially in emergency situations, users don' t know how to operate the system properly. Alarms can be activated by failing to close or lock doors and windows or by entering a secure area when the system is armed. In jurisdictions where police response is considered slow to minor situations, some merchants improperly use their alarm systems to summon the police to deal with non-emergent situations, such as bad checks or suspicious individuals.

Poor installation or servicing can also be a contributing factor in sending false alarms. For a system to function properly, it must first be installed properly and be well maintained. Equipment that is installed in the wrong environment or improperly positioned, set, or wired is prone to produce false alarms. Proper installation should include the proper repositioning or reinstalling when modifications to a facility (remodeling, additions, etc.) are made. The probability of false alarms increases the lack of proper system maintenance proportionately. The security consultant should be alert to installations and maintenance performed by personnel who lack the necessary skills and knowledge for today' s highly sophisticated equipment.

The results of poor installation and servicing coupled with resultant false alarms have prompted many states and local governments to establish standards for installing and servicing alarm systems. In addition to standards and regulations, the posting of a bond is now required in some jurisdictions. When conducting the security survey, the consultant should be attentive to all applicable rules, regulations, and standards. Assistance can usually be obtained from the jurisdiction within which the facility is located.

Faulty equipment is also a leading factor in causing false alarms. "Looking" for faulty equipment is a prime function of proper maintenance. All reputable alarm companies can and should offer test and inspection (T&I) services to their clients. The security consultant should be sure to review T&I records when conducting the security survey. Electrically or mechanically defective equipment can falsely activate a system by breaking or shorting a circuit.

The continued high incidence of false alarms, whatever the cause, has led to other problems. False alarms have been the cause of severe disruptions to public emergency service organizations. These disruptions have caused many jurisdictions to severely limit or eliminate the availability of direct notification systems. Automatic telephone dialer alarm systems, for example, are available only to restricted types of facilities in many jurisdictions. Others are required to have their direct systems monitored by private alarm companies that verify alarms prior to notifying emergency service agencies. Some jurisdictions impose fines or user fees upon users whose systems produce false alarms.

Emergency services personnel are placed at risk when responding to false alarms. Police and firefighters, as well as innocent bystanders, encounter dangers associated with high-speed response when responding to what they believe are legitimate emergencies. False alarms also divert emergency services personnel and may render them unavailable to respond to actual emergencies.

Monitoring Systems

Electronic monitoring and alarm systems are also used to monitor the functions of equipment and machinery for a variety of reasons. Alarms that monitor environmental conditions (temperature and water), for example, are used to protect sophisticated computer equipment from damage or shut-down caused by excessive heat or the introduction of water (leaks, etc.) There are many other processes and pieces of equipment critical to the continued operation of business. Often, this equipment needs to be monitored by an electronic system capable of sending an alarm in the case of a malfunction. Malfunctions can vary from the benign to the extremely urgent, such as an equipment failure in a nuclear power plant.

CCTV and other electronic surveillance equipment are complimentary additions to monitoring systems. CCTV provides remote overt or covert monitoring of an environment, equipment, or process without on-site personnel. CCTV is an effective loss prevention tool when applied in applications such as retail stores, warehouses, and areas of limited visibility. When used in conjunction with a video or digital recorder, CCTV provides a visual record (evidence) of the criminal act and assists in the identification of the perpetrators. CCTV systems are frequently used in industrial facilities, retail stores, hospitals, hotels, motels, banks, office buildings, and other areas.

The basic components of a CCTV system consist of a television camera, a monitor, connecting circuitry, and a power source. Although expensive, elaborate and expanded systems with numerous cameras, monitors, recorders, remote control, and other features are often cost-effective when considering the reduction in security personnel required and the resultant loss prevention advantage afforded, and may be much more cost-effective than other systems, depending on needs and application.

Access Control Systems

Controlling access and egress from facilities is a primary function of all security systems. Access control, as defined here, is an electronic means of controlling and monitoring the movement of people or vehicles in and out of secured areas. Access control systems are programmed to allow or disallow access to restricted places based on a number of criteria, i.e., time, personnel, day of week, frequency of access, etc. The system operates by a person introducing coded access cards, push button (combination) sequences, or a combination of both. The latest technology includes biometric sensors that verify fingerprints, handprints, eye images, or voice patterns and is used when the highest levels of security are required, i.e., classified government facilities, etc.

Good access control systems identify and record who passed through a protected area and when. These systems are computerized and provide immediate information about who gains access to the facility, where, and when.

When integrated with intrusion alarm systems, access points can generate alarm signals when doors or gates have been compromised by force, have been propped open, or left ajar.

Underwriters' Laboratories

Underwriters' Laboratories (UL) is a well-known, highly regarded, independent, non-profit service corporation that objectively applies existing safety and testing standards to products submitted by manufacturers. The UL label on a product is an indication that the equipment in question is of high quality and that the manufactured item meets strict UL standards. UL standards must be met for an alarm system to be certified. Protective devices, control units, circuitry, etc. must meet specific UL burglary prevention and detection standards to be installed in a certified system. In addition to the certification of alarm and detection devices, UL certifies local and central-station alarm service companies. Alarm installing companies and service companies must utilize UL-approved products, install alarm systems according to UL standards, provide maintenance and inspection as required, and satisfy certain performance standards for alarm responses. UL conducts periodic inspections of UL-listed monitoring stations.

Summary

The security consultant should have an understanding of the effective and efficient usage, applications, operations, and principles of electronic alarm systems. There are a wide variety of systems and devices available, and more are always being developed. All systems have weak points by which their functioning can be minimized, disrupted, or bypassed, yet most will prove satisfactory if properly selected, installed, and maintained.

Electronic access, warning, CCTV, and detection systems are beneficial in a wide variety of applications; however, security personnel should plan each application carefully and thoroughly analyze their security needs and the systems available before making a decision.

Chapter Seven

Security Storage and Information Security

Generally, the most highly secured unit within any facility is the high-security storage area. The nature of the business conducted, the levels of security clearance classification, and the items or valuables being protected will dictate the degree of desired security for any facility. Every facility has unique security requirements. The following are general principles that apply to all security programs.

The type and quality of security storage containers will depend on what is being protected. A security storage container for classified documents will be different from one for jewels or precious metals. Fire-resistant containers are more appropriate for paper documents, whereas a tamper- or burglary-resistant unit would be required for the jewels or precious metals.

Security storage containers are generally either fire-resistant or burglary-resistant but not always both. New advances in technology are addressing this, and many of the newer state-of-the-art security containers will provide a measure of protection against both fire and theft. However, most storage containers still usually provide only one specialized function and provide only minimum protection in the other area. Costs can be greatly reduced by purchasing a container that will serve only one function and provide only one type of protection.

Safes

Because they are usually expensive, careful attention must be given to the particular needs and application before selecting a safe. Safes fall into two categories that describe the degree of protection they provide: (1) fire-resistive and (2) burglary- and robbery-resistive. The fire protection rating of safes is established by the Safe Manufacturers National Association (SMNA) and independent tests conducted by Underwriter's Laboratories (UL).

Fire-Resistive Safes

SMNA provides technical specifications for the manufacturing of fire-resistant or resistive containers, and UL does the independent testing. The UL label or rating means that the safes in that class meet the minimum fire specifications designed for that class by SMNA.

Fire-resistive safes are double-walled or multiple-walled containers. Between the outer and inner metal walls are layers of moisture-impregnated insulation. When the safe is exposed to intense heat, the moisture is driven off in the form of steam, thus allowing for the dissipation of heat. Although locking devices for both fire-resistive and burglary-resistive safes are similar, the locking device itself has nothing to do with determining whether or not the unit is fire-resistive. The construction features and performance standards of the fire-resistive safe are such that little protection is provided against the safecracker. Once exposed to a fire, the inner insulation is usually destroyed, rendering a fire-resistant safe obsolete.

Burglary- and Robbery-Resistive Safes

Burglary-and robbery-resistive safes, commonly known as mercantile, money safes, or money chests, are classified by SMNA specifications and UL ratings, and are listed by insurance underwriters according to these classifications into their Mercantile Safe Policies.

Burglary-resistive safes are rated according to design features, including the thickness and type of metal, lock type, and performance standards. Most burglary-resistive safes have thick round or square steel doors and thick steel walls at least 1-½ inches thick. The performance standards determine the type of attack that the safe can withstand and for what length of time. As in any security device, delaying unauthorized access is nearly as important as preventing it.

Safecracking Methods

Modern, high-quality cutting and burning tools are effective in defeating most safes in use today, regardless of rating or quality. Skilled safecrackers armed with the best tools are still a serious security threat. If the safecracker has defeated or bypassed the perimeter barriers and alarm system, if any, there are several techniques available to him to attack the safe. Before attempting an attack on a safe, the professional safecracker studies the methods utilized to secure it. The skilled burglar will attempt to determine the safe' s combination and any access codes to gain entry into the facility. Employees, disgruntled employees, and former employees have frequently been identified as associates in a safecracking burglary. The two types of attack are force and without force.

Drilling and Punching

Lesser-quality locking mechanisms can be defeated by drilling, prying, or knocking off the combination dial, or by drilling a small hole near the combination dial to expose the locking device. Safes not equipped with relocking devices that jam the locking mechanism into place offer minimal resistance to this technique. When used to secure high-value items, this type of safe should only be used in conjunction with other security measures to afford appropriate levels of protection.

Burning

Oxyacetylene torches, more commonly known as cutting torches, are used to cut an opening in the wall or door of the safe. The burning method is intended to create an opening large enough to expose the locking mechanism or to remove the contents of the safe. A "thermic lance" is a device consisting of a hollow metal bar packed with ferrous alloy rods attached to an oxygen tank that feeds through the ferrous alloy rods. When lit with an acetylene torch, tremendous heat is generated, capable of burning through the toughest steel safe.

Ripping and Peeling

Some lesser-grade safes have doors or walls constructed of thin steel plates laminated or riveted together to create the door or wall. The safecracker opens this safe by prying the seams of these metal plates away from joints and seams using pry bars and other tools and "peels back" the layers of metal, exposing the locking mechanism or the interior of the safe. Ripping is accomplished against an inferior safe with thin solid metal outer or inner walls.

X-Ray

Portable x-ray machines used to examine the locking mechanism can reveal the position of the combination and the manipulation necessary to open the safe. This uncommon technique of safecracking may be defeated by the installation of shields allowing protection of the combination from x-ray.

Explosives

The introduction of more efficient and safer tools and techniques is responsible for a decline in using explosives as a means of safecracking. However, explosives like nitroglycerin and plastic explosives in the hands of someone well qualified to use them can still be used to "crack" a safe.

Power Tools

Power-driven rotary devices, hydraulic tools, and power drills equipped with carbide and diamond cutting surfaces, can be utilized to pry, cut, spread, peel, and drill openings into the door or body of the safe.

Summary

Other than x-ray and manipulation, safecracking involves forcible entry. Few safecrackers have the skill to manipulate the combination of a modern, high-quality safe without possessing some prior knowledge. Successful manipulation is usually the result of a burglar having discovered, stolen, or been given the combination to the safe.

No safe is totally safe! The old axiom "you get what you pay for" certainly applies to safes. The burglary-resistant properties provided by a safe are in direct proportion to its quality and cost.

As stated earlier, additional measures should be taken to provide for a safe's protection. Perimeter barriers, adequate locking hardware, electronic alarm systems, or other security procedures must be employed to achieve the highest levels of security. How a safe is used is just as important as its quality.

Safes should not be placed in remote, poorly lit locations within the facility. Rather, the safe should be placed where unauthorized access is likely to be discovered. Combinations and key inventory control must be strictly secured. As with other locking devices, the combinations and keys should be expertly changed regularly.

The security of a safe can frequently and easily be improved by taking simple steps to reduce its vulnerability. Industry standards dictate that all safes weighing less than 750 pounds should be anchored to the building structure, thus making its removal from the premises more difficult. For example, this is quite common when a fire-resistant safe is purchased and encased in concrete. This increases its fire-resistant qualities and also makes it less vulnerable to other safecracking techniques and removal.

The decision to purchase either a fire-resistive or burglary-resistive storage container must include consideration of its utilization and function as a protective device, business practices, risk factors, and environmental conditions.

Vaults

A vault is a room designed for the secure storage of valuables and is different from a safe in that it is larger, a part of the building structure, is constructed of different materials, and is designed to accommodate entry by one or more people. Effective vaults have walls, floors, and ceilings of reinforced concrete at least 12 inches in thickness. Vault doors should be made of thick steel or other torch- and drill-resistant material, be equipped with a combination lock, a firelock and lockable day gate, and be designed to afford an appropriate degree of fire protection.

Ratings for vaults are established by the Insurance Services Office (ISO) and are based on the type of construction materials utilized, their relative thickness, construction standards, and equipment features. All materials must be sufficiently thick for each rating category. Materials must be fabricated and installed according to established methods and standards. Construction standards and equipment features must be met in certain rating categories, such as inclusion of combination locks and time locks.

Electronic alarm protection and electronic access systems provide a greater measure of security and accountability. The use of an electronic access system in addition to the combination locks provides an audit trail of persons using the vault, and access is easily denied pending establishment of a new combination when needed.

Vault doors are protected by means of door contact switches and heat sensors. Some vault doors have a built-in wire grid that causes an alarm to sound if the wires are cut or melted. Additional protection of the vault can be provided by area or space devices, such as motion detectors, which react to anyone moving into the area around the vault, CCTV, and other high-tech applications.

When constructing vaults and other high-security "rooms" within an already secured facility, requirements outlined in Department of Defense (DOD) and Director, Central Intelligence (DCI) specifications can provide invaluable assistance. They will be mandatory if the government is the client.

Information Security

The security of records and information is absolutely vital to the effective continued operation of all organizations. The loss or destruction of such information or compromise of its confidentiality will likely result in one or more of the following:

- Interrupted production capability
- Loss of competitive edge in marketplace (loss of trade secrets, etc.)
- Inability to provide services or products
- Inability to satisfy certain legal requirements or contractual obligations
- Damaged dealings with suppliers and customers
- Financial harm to employees and stockholders

Obviously, the need to protect proprietary information is absolute!

Proprietary information comes in a variety of forms, and its relative importance varies from organization to organization. The first step in providing security and protection of information is to develop a procedure for the evaluation and control of information. At a minimum, the following steps must be taken in establishing an information-protection program:

- An ongoing inventory of all records, documents, and information
- The objective appraisal of the organizational value of the information, records, or documents
- Development of an information security-classification system
- Employ appropriate levels of security as determined by the information-classification system
- When the sources and types of information have been identified, a classification system must be developed to differentiate between vital and non-vital records. Different terms can be used to separate and identify the various

categories of information according to organizational value. One common example of classification is the following:

- Vital records that are essentially irreplaceable and are of the greatest value to the continued operation of the organization
- Important records that can only be replaced with great expense and inconvenience
- Useful records, which, when lost, would create inconveniences, but could be replaced rather quickly and inexpensively
- Nonessential records that are unessential to effective organizational operation

Other terms that could be used to categorize records are borrowed from the government: top secret, secret, confidential, etc., with the end product being the same, i.e., a system that implies the importance and composition of proprietary information.

Protective Measures

The protection of information is accomplished by procedural controls, duplication, and storage.

Procedural control applies to all aspects of security and especially so in information security. The process of information classification is the first step in controlling the flow of information through the organization. Controls must be established that limit the availability, responsibility, and accountability of information to personnel restricted or based only on "the need to know and the right to know." Organizational records must be secured and protected in descending order of importance—the more vital the record or information, the higher the level of control and security.

Duplication of records is both a security risk and a security asset. It serves as a backup to records that can be lost, stolen, or destroyed. It also provides the same information as the originals, thus requiring the same level of security as the originals. When copying documents and records, care must be exercised to prevent unauthorized duplication and the subsequent dissemination outside the organization. Duplicated vital records should be secured off-site to avoid loss to natural and man-made threats. Licensed and bonded classified-material storage companies offer this service to businesses.

Computer Security

Computer security begins with security of the hardware and extends to include the storage of information. The loss of a laptop, for example, is the loss of expensive hardware as well as the proprietary information contained therein. Strict accountability in the issuance of computers and requirements to utilize physical security measures to guard against hardware theft is critical.

Computer and information theft has become commonplace in business, industry, and government. Computers have greatly increased the ability to store, retrieve, manipulate, and transmit vital information. Accordingly, computers have become targets of theft. The misuse, damage, or loss of a computer can render helpless or even destroy an entire company. Electronic data-processing systems must be afforded a high level of security. Access to and operation of computer units must be strictly controlled. Attempts to enter, manipulate, or otherwise obtain information must be preventable and detectable.

Storage of data and programs on magnetic tapes, cards, discs, or drums is a vital part of any computer-security operation. Steps must be taken to provide security for the physical storage of tapes, cards, discs, etc. As with paper records, duplicated records should be secured off-site. Special storage units for the various data forms are available which provide not only security, but also a controlled environment.

Excessive heat and humidity in the storage unit or tape library can damage or destroy electronic information. Electronic access and alarm systems can monitor and alarm water levels and high temperatures, allowing for repairs to environmental control systems before damage occurs. Risks involving computers include fire, espionage, sabotage, accidental losses, theft, fraud, embezzlement, and natural disasters.

Summary

The security requirements of each facility must be established by considering and evaluating needs based on physical factors, type and extent of risk exposure, and business conducted. The effectiveness of a security program is measured in direct proportion to the decreases of the chances for criminal success. Information is a critical asset and must be protected accordingly. An in-depth evaluation of all records is mandatory in determining the appropriate level of security for the control of the flow and storage of information, records, documents— both paper and electronic.

Chapter Eight

Guard Services

Private security personnel now outnumber public law enforcement officers in the United States. Overburdened public law enforcement cannot and frequently will not provide security services to private enterprises. Growing crime rates and a public perception of out-of-control crime has established the need for extensive private security services in the private sector. A facility or organization that does not project a perception of security does not have adequate security! Security is as much a perception as it is a reality. Employees who feel vulnerable and insecure will be every bit as restless and non-productive as the employee who actually doesn' t have security in his or her workplace. This need for security has caused Americans to demand greater levels of personal and physical security. The security consultant will most likely be evaluating or otherwise be involved with security guards and guard companies. Accordingly, this chapter will discuss an overview of the security guard.

Current Industry Criticism

The private security industry is frequently criticized, and a good deal of that criticism is valid. At the same time, criticism leveled at the public criminal justice system has grown. The professions, especially teaching, law, and medicines, have also become more criticized recently. Therefore, private security personnel should not be overly reactive in their response to criticism. They, like all professionals, should simply strive to increase their personal and industrial professional development.

Recent studies conducted of the age, race, education, and general physical characteristics of private security personnel have found that the differences between private and public law enforcement, on these factors, are "minimal."

Despite these studies, security guards, perhaps due to their low salaries or minimal qualifications, frequently are the subjects of investigations when criminal activity is suspected within a facility or organization. Unfortunately, this suspicion is often founded.

When an international Fortune 500 company experienced the theft of nearly sixty laptop computers in one summer month, an investigation resulted in the identification, arrest, and successful prosecution of the perpetrator— a security guard. However, it is also true that a high-level manager was identified in the theft of one computer. In this case, there was no arrest or prosecution.

This is a pitfall that the security consultant must be aware of— sometimes the corporate thinking is "only cleaning ladies and security guards can be thieves." High earners for the corporation, on the other hand, can do no wrong. Be cautious!

Recruitment

Job seekers looking for positions as security guards and security officers will likely find that newspaper advertisements and listings of contract security companies in the Yellow Pages provide the best leads for employment opportunities. In papers throughout the United States, especially in and near cities, there are ads placed by companies seeking applicants. Traditional qualifications for employment, such as education and experience, are seldom listed. About the only general qualification is a "clean police record," which certainly should be expected. Unfortunately, there is often little agreement in the industry about what is considered a "clean record," and what is acceptable to one employer might not be acceptable to another. Most security firms in major cities maintain full-time employment offices.

The recruitment of management personnel is a different process. Companies fill these positions by promoting from within or by recruiting persons from the outside. Many recruited from outside the company come from the ranks of public law enforcement. Frequently, former law enforcement personnel are attractive to security companies for two reasons: their skills and their contacts.

Another recruiting source used is campus recruitment. In many cases, security companies recruit directly with college criminal justice departments, while some companies simply utilize established general college recruitment processes.

The recruitment of security personnel is not a complex or sophisticated process, and coupled with the high turnover rate of over 100 percent per year, is one of the main problems and biggest weaknesses in the industry.

Selection

There are no industry-wide selection standards for security guards. State and local laws have recently established minimum standards in some cases, but they are just that— minimal. Many government studies and writers on the subject have indicated there should be minimum qualifications for selection, similar to those used in public law enforcement.

There is little hope that this will happen, for several reasons. First, private security is a competitive business, and any set selection standards would tend to reduce the pool of, and increase competition for, available applicants. Security employers fear that this supply-and-demand situation will raise salary levels and make it harder for them to sell their services.

Second, unless all private security employers agreed to or were mandated to accept set selection standards, the only recourse would be legislation, controlled through licensing and registration by the state. Most companies view this as government interference and strongly oppose it.

The screening process is another weak point in the selection of personnel. Many applicants begin their employment within one to two days after making application. The industry defends this practice by insisting that they will observe the employee's performance carefully and that the best judgment of their qualifications will be their work performance.

Security consultants familiar with the private security guard industry realize this rationale is weak. Most companies are in immediate need of security guard personnel and are unwilling, partially because of the turnover rate, to invest the time and money to thoroughly screen applicants. To increase professionalism in the security guard industry, more effective and comprehensive recruitment procedures must be established. The following are recommended minimal recruitment procedures.

Screening Interview

A face-to-face, two-way screening interview between the employer and the applicant is a must. Although somewhat subjective, a properly conducted interview by a skilled interviewer will likely identify the applicant's weaknesses.

The interviewer should clearly communicate the requirements, positive and negative aspects, salary and fringe benefits, and other pertinent factors about the position and the company. The skilled interviewer will gain insight into the applicant's character at this time. Although this assessment is subjective, the applicant's demeanor and attitude during the interview may indicate the need for more careful background investigation.

Honesty Test

State and federal laws pertaining to employment should be carefully examined prior to using written honesty tests or polygraph examinations. In some jurisdictions, the polygraph is permitted for use in personnel selection in restricted industries, such as public law enforcement and private security. Honesty tests refer only to written tests that allow employers to gain insights into a prospective employee's honesty without extensive costs. Honesty tests are designed to measure trustworthiness, attitude toward honesty, and the need to steal.

Background Investigation

It might be said that the background investigation (BI) is the most boring and least exciting type of assignment an investigator can receive. It can also be said that it is perhaps the most valuable and important investigation that will be conducted. BIs frequently stop trouble before it starts. Background investigations must be conducted prior to employment or assignment.

All too often, employers do not conduct any background investigations, or investigations are minimal and conducted by non-investigative personnel. As in the recruitment process, many security guards are hired and assigned within one to two days of making their application. *No* complete BI can be conducted in that short a time frame. Many employers use only the telephone or form letters for background information. Such methods do not provide adequate data for effective verification and evaluation.

Whenever possible, field investigations should be conducted to obtain valuable information about an individual's character and ability that cannot be gained by other means.

Other Screening Considerations

Extensive background investigations, job-related psychological tests, and detection-of-deception examinations should be considered when employing personnel with fiduciary responsibilities, access to children, access to arms, or other sensitive assignments. Job factors, such as access to funds and other property, control of personnel, whether armed, and so forth, should determine the types of job-related tests that can best serve the employer and the public. It is shocking to realize that many armed guards are not screened to determine if they have major psychological problems that would clearly render them unacceptable for employment involving carrying a deadly weapon.

Training

Training always has been and always will be a major problem in the security guard industry. Few employers provide any training beyond what is required by state or local law. There is probably no more important issue in private security today than formal training or the lack of it.

Perhaps the most significant difference between private security and public law enforcement is the issue of training. While most states require entry level and in-service comprehensive training programs for law enforcement officers, few have similar requirements for the private security industry. A distinction must be made in the selection and training between armed and unarmed personnel.

Licensing and Registration

Private security executives have begun to recognize the need for some type of government regulation to ensure uniformity of requirements. There is no unanimity on the issue of who should be the "regulator." There is, however, industry-wide agreement that it should not be the same agency that regulates public law enforcement. To be effective, licensing and registration requirements must be established that are equitable and established jointly by industry professionals with some input from the public law enforcement community.

Security Guard Duties

This is a rather complex issue, due to the wide variety of duties and functions performed by employees in the broad category of "private security personnel." In addressing this issue, the Private Security Task Force emphasized the need for job descriptions for private security personnel. The task force found, as a general guide, the data recorded in job descriptions should relate to two essential features of each position:

- The nature of the work involved
- The employee type who appears best fitted for the position

Guard and patrol services include the provision of personnel who perform the following functions, either contractually or internally, at such places and facilities as industrial plants, financial institutions, educational institutions, office buildings, retail establishments, commercial complexes (including hotels and motels), health care facilities, recreation facilities, libraries and museums, residence and housing developments, charitable institutions, transportation vehicles and facilities (public and common carriers), and warehouses and goods distribution depots:

- Prevention and detection of intrusion, unauthorized entry or activity, vandalism, or trespass on private property
- Prevention and detection of theft, loss, embezzlement, misappropriation or concealment of merchandise, money, bonds, stocks, notes, or other valuable documents or papers
- Control, regulation, or direction of the flow or movements of the public, whether by vehicle or otherwise, to assure the protection of property
- Protection of individuals from bodily harm
- Enforcement of rules, regulations, and policies related to crime reduction

These functions may be provided at one location or several. Guard functions are generally provided at one central location for one client or employer. Patrol functions, however, are performed at several locations, often for several clients.

Chapter Nine

The Criminal Threat

Internal

The impact of thefts and other problems initiated by employees on business and other organizations has reached alarming proportions. These loses are frequently passed on to the consumers and taxpayers. White-collar crimes, including fraud and embezzlement, account for major losses in various enterprises. Without proper oversight and other safeguards, fraud frequently remains undetected until serious damage has already occurred. Some companies continue to refer to internal losses as "shortages" rather than attempt to detect and deter internal crime.

Embezzlement

Embezzlement is a fraud perpetrated by an insider who has access to money or property and the ability to conceal the theft by "burying" it in paperwork. For example, a simple embezzlement could be the "hiding" of an unauthorized credit card purchase among many, perhaps hundreds, of legitimate receipts.

Insurance industry studies reveal losses from embezzlement of cash reserves are seven to ten times higher than losses from property or merchandise. The security consultant must distinguish between the simple theft of property and merchandise from embezzlement. Only more skilled thieves will be effective in large-scale embezzlement of property.

To reduce the risk of embezzlement, employers and security consultants must be familiar with the human and physical elements that are generally present in embezzlement: need, rationalization, and opportunity.

Need – Unusual or excessive debts may cause an employee to consider converting merchandise or money to his or her own use. Security consultants and employers should be alert to telltale signs, such as employees who live beyond their means. Personal financial gain represents the major reason why employees steal from their employer. Because the psychological needs of individuals are difficult to discover and change over time, it is virtually impossible to identify unsatisfied needs and therefore prevent embezzlement.

Rationalization – Rationalization is the subconscious psycho-logical state that provides explanations and excuses for one's inappropriate acts. Rationalizations may include:

- I'm "borrowing, not stealing"
- Lack of moral restraint: "I can't help it"
- Moral right: "they owe me"
- Reward: "I earned it"

The "borrowing, not stealing" rationalization occurs when the employee tells himself that he will return the money. Sometimes, the employee may return the money in the beginning, but as the ease increases, with repeated thefts combined with growing amounts too large to repay, it becomes more unlikely that the employee will or can repay.

Lack of moral restraint rationalization happens when an employee believes it is "ok" because others are doing it too. The moral right rationalization occurs when an employee believes he is only taking "what they owe me." The reward rationalization is somewhat a combination of the lack of moral restraint and the moral right rationalization—the employee sees other workers stealing and not getting caught and "believes" it is owed him anyway.

Opportunity – Certain conditions must exist for the act of embezzlement to occur. Opportunity presents itself through lax or nonexistent controls and procedures. Strict accountability and other controls must be in place to detect and deter embezzlement. Eliminating opportunity is the key to controlling the elements of need and rationalization. The lack of opportunity will never eliminate the need to embezzle, but it can prevent the act from happening.

Employers and security consultants should be vigilant in their observation of behavioral conditions that may implicate an employee involved in embezzlement. The most significant behavioral condition is the employee living beyond his means, making sudden changes in spending habits, and making large and excessively expensive purchases.

Also, an employer should be aware of employees who have suffered major illness or a member of the immediate family has had such an illness and a large indebtedness occurred. Second, employees who handle large amounts of money or approve purchases and vendor contracts should be observed and required to adhere to corporate policies. Employees with fiduciary functions who strongly object to procedural changes or closer supervision should be audited or observed. Their resistance may be an indication of their fear of discovery of an illegal act.

Fraud

Fraud is defined as the intentional perversion of truth for the purpose of inducing another in reliance upon it to part with something of value belonging to him or to surrender a legal right. Fraud is an essential element in various statutory offenses involving theft, misappropriation, and inventory shrinkage. Fraud includes all acts, omissions, and concealments that involve a break of legal or equitable trust or confidence and are injurious to another.

Some examples of fraud are: money being paid by a third person to a clerk for the clerk's employer and the clerk appropriates it or part of it before it is put in the cash register. Another example is where a manufacturer is a delivering product and the employee misappropriates or diverts some or all of the goods to his own use.

Pilferage

Pilferage is the stealing of property of another in small amounts over a long period of time. Items taken are relatively inexpensive and, on a one-time basis, are almost insignificant. Cumulatively, incidents of pilferage by one or more employees can amount to enormous losses to the organization. No one actually knows how large the employee pilferage problem is or what portion of inventory shrinkage can be attributed to dishonest employees.

Estimates on the number of employees who steal vary anywhere from five percent to seventy-five percent of the workforce. The opportunity to embezzle and perpetrate other frauds is restricted to a small percentage of employees. Accordingly, the greater number of employees who steal do so by committing simple acts of pilferage.

Employee pilferage schemes are likely to be simple, as little planning and preparation is needed to steal company property. Studies have shown that people are more likely to steal from businesses and organizations than from other people.

Theft-Control Strategies

Employers must make all employees aware that internal thefts are a serious problem and that they will not be tolerated. In the interest of business and honest employees, employers must take some action on a regular basis to detect and deter dishonest acts by employees. To reduce losses to theft, many employers use in-house security, contract guard services, and various types of surveillance equipment. The purpose of these security measures is to eliminate the opportunity to commit theft by monitoring and restricting the movement of employees and visitors (vendors and contractors) in and about the facility.

Opportunity reduction can be accomplished through closer supervision, enforcement of procedural and access controls, increased use of security hardware devices, and increased emphasis on security and its importance at all levels of the workforce.

The employer should develop and implement at least the following four strategies for reducing and controlling internal theft losses:

- Screening of applicants,
- Procedures or devices that make theft more difficult or apprehension easier,
- Improvement in employee satisfaction, and
- The policy and process of apprehension and prosecution.

Many companies frown on strict enforcement of security programs as a perceived invasion of personal rights. The security consultant must not be swayed in his quest to recommend appropriate security measures. As previously stated, I believe security is as much perception as it is reality. Once a company with lax or nonexistent security programs is victimized, employee morale will soon suffer. Many "bosses" feel personally violated when trusted employees victimize the company.

Restoration or establishment of appropriate—not overreacting or knee-jerking—security measures must be made to return the workplace and workforce to a "normal" and acceptable level of comfort, productivity, and security. Once the security consultant can tactfully demonstrate to the employer what went wrong, appropriate recommendations will be more readily accepted.

Security procedures and devices utilized by any organization must be directed to reducing the opportunity for crime. The organizational environment, regardless of its function, is not safe or secure and will not be perceived by employees to be so if it is subjected to employee theft.

Security programs should be fair, equitable, and balanced to prevent negative effects on employee morale and productivity. Security programs that treat different "classes" of employees differently will soon create a negative "them and us" mentality among the lower-paid categories of employees and may generate the very problems it was designed to prevent.

Security programs involving apprehension and prosecution must have a solid foundation. Security personnel must be properly trained and supervised if they are to be vested with this responsibility. Unfortunately, some organizations doubt the cost involved in a solid security program is worth its deterrent effect. The rate of prosecution of employee thieves is extremely low and the decision to prosecute is not always up to the organization.

The decision not to prosecute may often be the most appropriate. Prosecution by its very nature is fraught with risk. The arrest and prosecution of a high-ranking financial executive for fraud or embezzlement, for example, is a "slippery slope." Management may desire to send a message that this behavior will not be tolerated and may be seeking restitution.

On the other hand, an arrest of this nature is likely to generate adverse press—stockholders don't want to see this in the *Wall Street Journal* . A decision to prosecute may ultimately lead to a need to defend against libel and malicious-prosecution civil suits. Additionally, other expenses may arise, such as having security employees, supervisors, managers, and witnesses available in court and a willingness to indemnify the employees involved in these cases if a civil suit or complaint involves them personally.

External

Employee crime generally has a far greater financial impact on the organization than crimes committed by individuals outside the organization. External crime is still responsible for enormous dollar losses, however, and "outsiders" are more likely than employees to perpetrate crimes against persons.

Robbery

Robbery is defined as the taking or attempting to take anything of value from the care, custody, or control of a person or persons by force, threat of force or violence, or by putting the victim in fear.

Criminologists believe that robbers plan their crimes to some extent. The robber usually wants easy money quickly and will look for a soft target that offers little resistance and a minimum of exposure and risk. As previously discussed, it is the security function to "harden" the targets. Effective employment of security personnel, lighting, barriers, access systems, alarms, surveillance equipment, and other measures will result in sending a message to the would-be robber—Don' t do it here or you will be identified and apprehended. In other words, deny the robber the opportunity to ply his trade.

The most serious aspect of a robbery is the violence, hence, a crime against persons. Many, perhaps one in five victims of commercial robbery, suffer injury or death at the hands of robbers. Most robbery victims that were injured or killed offered some degree of resistance. Employees should receive at least a minimum of training on how to react to crime. Employees should be instructed to:

- Do whatever it takes to stay alive; money and merchandise has no value if you are dead.
- Advise the robber that you will cooperate.
- Remember that once a robbery is in progress, it is too late for preventive measures and the employee can't stop it.
- Remain as calm as possible.
- Concentrate on what the robber wants and what you are to do to satisfy the robber.
- Discreetly observe the robber and look for general characteristics of height, weight, race, sex, weapon, clothing, and mode of travel as well as specific characteristics like tattoos, scars, missing teeth, and speech impediments.
- As soon as the robber has left the premises and you are safe, immediately call the police. Do not notify anyone else before calling the police.

To reduce or prevent robberies, businesses must plan and implement robbery prevention policies and procedures. Effective robbery prevention saves lives and property and prevents serious injuries.

Burglary

Burglary is defined as the unlawful entry of, or remaining in, a structure to commit a crime therein. The degree of burglary is categorized by a number of aggravating factors: armed, unarmed, forcible entry, unlawful entry where no force is used, and attempted forcible entry. Burglary is the second most-prevalent property crime in the United States.

As with robbery, burglary is more likely and more prevalent in "soft" targets. Burglary is a serious felony crime that has great potential to evolve into a crime against persons if unsuspecting victims are on the premises during a burglary. Hard targets will reduce the burglar's impulse to commit the crime.

As described in other chapters, the best overall strategy is to ensure that likely entry points are safely guarded by physical and visible means of discouragement. The employment of security personnel, access and alarm systems, lights, locks, CCTV, fencing, and barriers making entry appear difficult and detection and apprehension likely is called "target hardening." The security systems should make it difficult and time-consuming to burglarize the building. The use of silent alarms activated by the intrusion improves the chances of apprehending the violator. Marking merchandise with highly visible and unique markings makes the merchandise harder to fence and easier to trace and identify, thus reducing its value to the intruder.

Burglars are mostly young males and can be placed into three general categories: the amateur, the semiprofessional, and the professional.

Amateurs comprise over two-thirds of all known burglars and are usually looking for a "soft" target of opportunity. Professional preventive steps will make a target too difficult for the amateur.

Semiprofessional burglars comprise about one-third of known burglars and pose the greatest immediate threat to a business. The semipro will not be deterred by a weak security system of mediocre lights, locks, or alarms, and generally has ties to a fence to dispose of stolen property.

Professional burglars makeup less than 2 percent of the known population of burglars and pose the greatest long-term threat to a business. The true professional can pick locks, bypass alarms, turn off lighting systems, and open safes and is usually only interested in obtaining extremely large amounts of money or valuable merchandise that is small in size. The professional is deterred by reducing the amount of money or merchandise available on the premises in addition to the employment of highly sophisticated security hardware. All security systems should be designed to delay the burglar, regardless of his degree of skill—the longer he is delayed, the more likely he is to go elsewhere.

The police should be called prior to entering a building if a burglary or burglary attempt has been discovered. Crucial evidence needed to identify and apprehend the perpetrator may be irrevocably lost if the crime scene is compromised in any way. Additionally, it could be dangerous for company employees to enter a building that could be harboring the burglar.

Shoplifting

Retail stores are the most vulnerable to shoplifting and theft of small, easily concealed items. Grocery, hardware, drug, and general merchandising stores carry items that are easily stolen.

Most shoplifters are amateurs who operate alone and are likely to steal as a part of ordinary customer behavior. Studies have shown that shoplifters usually operate when stores are crowded or in stores they consider soft targets. These are stores where employees are not trained and are unfamiliar with shoplifting techniques. Fridays, Saturdays, and holidays are usually the big days for shoplifting because they represent a time when stores are crowded and store personnel are busy.

The two most serious problems associated with shoplifting are detecting the crime and dealing with the apprehended shoplifter. As with all crime prevention, it is much better to have a program to reduce the opportunity for shoplifting than to place an emphasis on the detection and apprehension of offenders. However, the detection and apprehension of shoplifters must be a part of a comprehensive security program.

There are three times that offer opportunities for control:

- When perpetrators enter the store
- When they pick up the merchandise
- When they leave the store

At the entrance, steps should be taken to intimidate shoplifters: high-visibility CCTV, warning signs, electronic sensor systems, or a reduction in their capability to conceal merchandise by requiring shoppers to check parcels at the counter.

Alert store employees should offer discreet, courteous intervention by offering assistance to shoplifters in the vicinity of their target merchandise. This technique puts shoplifters on notice that they are being watched and often causes them to leave the store. After shoplifters have concealed merchandise and are leaving, electronic sales tag sensors can either detect the presence of hidden goods or prompt the shoplifter to pay rather than risk detection.

Bad Checks and Credit Card Fraud

Checks – Bad check fraud covers things from accidental overdrafts against legitimate accounts to and including complex schemes to defraud, including check kiting, theft by deception, checks uttered against nonexistent and fraudulent accounts, insufficient funds, forgeries, and stolen checks. Bad check fraud costs the consumer and businesses many millions of dollars each year. The dollar amount of the fraud determines whether the offense is a misdemeanor or a felony. Prosecution of fraudulent check cases usually are based on checks uttered against nonexistent and fraudulent accounts, forgeries, and stolen checks.

Businesses receiving checks on a frequent basis should implement procedures to reduce the risk of receiving bad checks. Each business should establish a check cashing policy, advertise it, and enforce it:

- Know the customer or client. Obtain proper photo identification.
- Compare all personal information on the check with identification.
- Record identifying information from identification on the check, i.e., driver's license number, etc.

Many stores can benefit from establishing a "check cashing card" program that requires a person to file an application to receive a check-cashing card.

Compare the numerical amount against the written amount. Banks are obligated to honor the written amount on a check; make sure that the two amounts are the same.

Be cautious of "stale" dates and don't accept post-dated checks. Require explanations for checks more than thirty days old.

If signature is questionable, have the person sign again and compare to known signatures, i.e., photo ID, etc.

If you have further questions, verify the account with the bank. The bank's phone number and the checking account number are on all checks.

Checks returned marked "no account" or "closed account" should be taken as a warning of carelessness or possible fraud. Such a check is usually evidence of a fraud. If restitution is not made, prosecution would be appropriate. Forged checks are worthless, and using a forged check to pay for merchandise or services is a felony. Other alterations, illegal signatures, forgeries of the endorsement, erasures, or obliteration on genuine checks are also crimes. Dirty, damaged, and smudged checks and those with misspellings or other irregularities should be considered suspicious.

Credit Cards – Credit card fraud perpetrated by internal and external sources is a growing problem facing businesses today. Credit card fraud is responsible for greater losses to banks than check fraud.

Businesses that issue credit cards to their employees should establish strict corporate policy regarding their use and should conduct thorough credit checks on the individual before issuing a credit card.

Employees should be required to match their credit card receipts to comprehensive expense reports and to credit card company invoices. Employees should also be required to write a "brief note" on the back of the credit card receipt at the time of use to avoid a later failure to "recall" what the purchase was actually for and to know how to post the expense: sales, entertainment, supplies, equipment, etc.

Fraudulent credit card schemes include cards intentionally obtained from issuers with the intent to defraud, stolen from the mail, homes, offices, individuals, and using counterfeit, altered, and previously canceled cards. Credit card crimes are defined as theft and forgery, and may be related to other criminal acts committed in obtaining the cards, such as burglary, robbery, theft, mail fraud, and others.

The most effective measures for preventing credit card fraud are comparing purchase signatures with those on the card in addition to verifying the card's validity with the credit card company and insisting upon proper identification.

Bombs and Bomb Threats

Bombs and bombing is the preferred weapon of the terrorist. Bombs cause spectacular events resulting in the terrorists' much-desired attention by the media. Bombing is relatively easy and safe for the perpetrator. After setting a devise, the actor may simply walk away to safety. Due to the nature and extent of damage caused by a bomb, bombings are extremely difficult to investigate and require the services of experts, i.e., BATF, sophisticated police explosive ordinance units, and the military. Bombing is usually highly discriminate; that is, the target of a bomb is not often selected at random.

Bombs and bomb threats pose a serious problem. Management, especially of large multinational corporations, must establish bomb threat response as part of their security program. The bomb threat policy must consider the degree of risk and danger to personnel, the consequences of damaging or destroying materials in a facility, and the total cost or loss that would result from a bombing or bomb threat.

Bomb Threats

The first step in responding to a bomb threat is knowing what to do when the threat is received. The professional security consultant should have comprehensive, up-to-date reference materials. Included in that reference material should be information relating to bombs and bombers. The Bureau of Alcohol, Tobacco, and Firearms (BATF), Postal Inspection Service, U.S. Customs Service, and U.S. Army Ordinance Disposal are excellent sources of informational materials. BATF offers a handy and comprehensive pamphlet entitled "BOMB and Physical Security Planning" that is a must-read for the security professional.

Dealing with bombs and bomb threats is dealt with in greater detail in Chapter 11, "Emergency and Disaster Control."

Terrorism and Kidnapping

Terrorism, or rather the elements of terrorism, is a crime. Terrorism is the use or threatened use of force or violence used to coerce, demoralize, intimidate, or subjugate persons, organizations, businesses, or governments in order to obtain a political goal or philosophy. Slight variations exist in the official definitions of terrorism between such agencies as the FBI and U.S. State Department. Regardless of its "official definition," terrorism for our purposes is violence or the threat of violence against a client's personnel or facilities. For a number of reasons, both political and financial, American businesses are prime targets of terrorist organizations in many parts of the world.

American businesses, especially international and multinational companies, have been forced to establish anti-terrorist and counter-terrorist plans, which include the possibility of paying a ransom if an employee is kidnapped.

Most American law enforcement and security organizations are unfamiliar with counter-terror tactics, and assistance from local law enforcement agencies will be limited. The FBI has primary jurisdiction for terrorism within the United States. The U.S. State Department is the lead agency for terrorism overseas. Within the United States, the FBI has teamed up with local police agencies creating anti-terrorism task forces in such cities as New York. Law enforcement agencies have been extremely successful in investigating kidnappings in the United States. Following the September 11 attacks, President George W. Bush appointed former Pennsylvania Governor Tom Ridge as the first Director of Homeland Security with the daunting task of fostering communication, coordination, and cooperation among the federal law enforcement agencies performing terrorism counteraction duties. Corporate security organizations should form Crisis Management Teams (CMT) with responsibility for responding to terrorism threats against the company. The CMT has the following functions in the handling of terrorist threats:

- **Leadership** – Establishing the input and direction from senior management through a CMT liaison person
- **Security personnel** – Supplying expertise in resource protection and intelligence regarding terrorist organizations
- **Law department** – Providing legal counsel on the legal implications of CMT strategies and tactics
- **Financial** – Develops the financial base for CMT and records and documents all expenditures
- **Human resources and medical** – Provides the necessary health and biographical data on personnel and their families in the corporate framework
- **Media relations** – Provides the expertise to respond to the media
- **Adversary communications** – Exchanges information with the terrorists
- **Crisis counsel** – Works in conjunction with security to provide accurate and timely intelligence on the terrorist organizations involved in the crisis

Espionage and Sabotage

The loss of trade secrets can be devastating to companies of all sizes and descriptions. Trade secrets are defined by the company What one large company might deem as insignificant may very well be critically important to a small company. Frequently, businesses consider their customer lists confidential trade secrets. These companies spend time, money, and other resources developing their clients and cannot afford to have them fall into the wrong hands.

On the other end of the spectrum, confidential formulas, business plans, financial records, experimental development, and the like are trade secrets and are the "backbone" of the business. Every corporation has some trade secrets or confidential information that it must keep out of the hands of competitors. This is much more difficult for international corporations because trade secrets illegally obtained in this country may be perfectly legal and an acceptable business practice in a foreign country that does not recognize our laws pertaining to such incidents.

Disloyal employees or outsiders may commit espionage or sabotage. Multinational corporations have employees from a variety of nations, and the loyalty of such employees should be suspect when compared with loyalty for his or her native country and the type of business culture native to the employee. Industrial espionage is easily accomplished through the use of common business equipment: computers, cameras, copiers, and electronic listening and recording devices.

Sabotage and espionage pose two major threats:

- Threats against personal safety.
- Disruption of vital services.

Sabotage may be targeted against property and may not target people. Other actions, such as arson, may directly affect human life.

Sabotage can be defined as the intentional destruction of property. The saboteur, whether a professional or an amateur, may be recognized as an internal or external threat. The saboteur may work alone or with others. Many techniques and devises may be employed to commit sabotage, including:

- Arson – Fire and explosive devices
- Mechanical sabotage – Equipment and machinery rendered inoperative by tampering or intentionally poor maintenance

- Electrical and public utilities – Interruption of electrical, water, sewage, telecommunications, and other public services
- Contamination – The introduction of hazardous or toxic materials into drinking water supplies, air handling systems, fuel supplies, etc.
- Psychological – Disruptions based on human behaviors, such as labor disputes, disorderly conduct, etc. creating negative situations in the workplace

Sabotage and espionage are real threats to government and industry alike. Accordingly, security measures must be in place to safeguard information by controlling access and preventing unauthorized duplication and dissemination.

Summary

External threats and crimes pose a greater risk of injury or death than do internal threats and crimes, and although internal threat poses a greater risk for financial harm; the safeguarding against external threats and the protection of personnel must take precedence.

As businesses face increasing competition and rapidly changing technology, the preservation and protection of classified information and material becomes increasingly critical.

Chapter Ten

Fire Protection

Fire safety, prevention, and suppression is a complex science. This chapter is designed to provide the security consultant with a basic understanding of the relationship between the security and fire safety functions. The management of an organization has a responsibility to develop and implement programs in security, safety, and fire prevention with the goals of protecting life and property and to prevent, reduce, or eliminate company loss. These functions are often combined into one major department, or they may operate as individual, cooperative units within the company.

Characteristics of Fire

Fire is a major threat to life and property in any business, and all security employees should therefore be aware of the fundamentals of fire and fire protection. Fire is defined as rapid oxidation accompanied by heat and light. Three things must be present in sufficient quantities to sustain a fire: heat, fuel, and oxygen. This is referred to as the "fire triangle." When one or more elements of the triangle are removed, the fire will extinguish.

Oxygen

Oxygen is usually drawn from the air, but may be artificially introduced. Because oxygen is readily available from the air, eliminating or reducing it as a factor of combustion is often impractical. However, if oxygen supplies can be diminished or eliminated, the fire will be diminished or eliminated as well. Closing the door in an airtight vault, for example, will contain and ultimately extinguish a fire contained therein. Extinguishing agents can also be introduced to diminish the supply of oxygen and "smother" the fire.

Heat

Heat for ignition can come from many sources. The amount, or degree, of heat needed to cause combustion varies depending on the type of fuel present. For combustion to occur, most materials must be heated to the combustion temperature and, once begun, burning will continue as long as the fuel remains above this temperature and adequate supplies of fuel and oxygen remain.

Removing or diminishing the heat side of the fire triangle offers many ways to prevent and extinguish fires. The most common extinguishing agent used lower a fuel's ignition temperature is water. The introduction of water can also, when applied in copious amounts, disrupt the fuel supply, aiding in extinguishing a fire.

Fuel

Fuels come in three forms: solid, liquid, and gas. As discussed, eliminating the supply of fuel will extinguish a fire. This could be something as simple as closing a valve or something too complex to achieve. To successfully suppress a fire, one or more parts of the fire triangle must be removed or significantly diminished.

The best protection against fire is prevention. Management and safety and security personnel must understand the characteristics and nature of fire in order to take those steps necessary to prevent the creation of a fire hazard.

Security's Role

Security may have either a direct or indirect organizational responsibility for the development, operation, and enforcement of a fire safety program. Established security programs assist in fire safety by facilitating and controlling the movement of persons in the facility, ensuring orderly conduct on the property, and protecting life and property at all times. Security operations should provide the following in support of the fire safety program:

- Prevent unauthorized access to persons who might set a fire
- Control the activities of people authorized to be on the property and assist anyone who may not be aware of fire safety policies
- Control pedestrian and vehicular traffic during fire drills and evacuation during actual emergencies
- Control of roads, gates, driveways and vehicular traffic to facilitate access by the fire and police departments
- Check conditions of "hot work," including cutting and welding, and if necessary, prepare to operate fire-extinguishing equipment
- Practice diligence in observing conditions likely to cause a fire
- Routine examinations of firefighting equipment, extinguishers, sprinkler systems, etc.
- Perform tests of firefighting equipment and conduct fire drills
- Operate fire control equipment after giving the alarm and before the response of others persons to the fire
- Monitor fire alarm signals and detection systems
- Ensure patrol routes provide surveillance of potential fire hazards

Security guard post orders should include:

- Ensure that doors, gates, windows, skylights, fire doors, and fire shutters are closed and locked properly.

- Ensure the removal or proper storage of combustible materials: waste, rags, paint residue, rubbish, etc.
- Ensure that all fire apparatus is in place and accessible.
- Ensure that exits and aisles are clear and exit signs are properly posted and functional.
- Secure machinery carelessly left running.
- Check the facility for carelessly discarded smoking materials.
- Check space heaters.
- Ensure that hazardous manufacturing and operating procedures are maintained in a safe condition.
- Check sprinkler-valve pressure gauges.
- Check for proper operation of heating, ventilation, and air conditioning equipment (HVAC).
- Close leaking air and water valves.
- Carefully patrol areas of renovation and new construction; be alert to fire and safety threats.
- Record and report violations of safety and security policies; ensure repairs to dangerous situations.

Training for Fire Prevention and Protection

Security personnel must be thoroughly acquainted with the property they are protecting and the policies, procedures, and programs implemented to guide them in their duties. Security personnel must be familiar with the physical features of the property, the materials utilized and stored on the premises, the fire suppression and detection equipment and materials, their location, and proper operation. Proper training for security personnel should include the classes of fire, basic first aid, extinguishing agents and equipment, and available support services.

Hazardous Material

Hazardous materials include:

- Flammable gases

- Materials subject to spontaneous heating and ignition
- Explosive materials, acids, and oxidizing agents
- Flammable and combustible liquids
- Combustible dust
- Light combustibles, wood, paper, etc.

Classes of Fire

The four classes of fire, as defined by the fuel type:

- Class A – Common combustibles: wood, paper, clothing, rubber, and some plastics
- Class B – Flammable liquids: petroleum-based gas and oil products, etc.
- Class C – Electrical equipment
- Class D – Combustible metals: sodium, magnesium, and potassium, etc.

To properly and effectively suppress a fire, it is important to accurately define its fuel source. A basic knowledge of the combustibles is needed to select the proper extinguishing agent.

Classes of Extinguishers

Fire extinguishers are designed to discharge a specific type of fire-extinguishing agent. Effectiveness depends on using the proper extinguisher and extinguishing agent for the fire encountered. Some extinguishers are effective on only one type of fire, while others are suitable for two or more classes of fire. Fire extinguishers are classified as A, B, C, or D according to the class of fire they are designed to extinguish.

- Class A extinguishers are heat absorbing and are used to extinguish common combustible fires. They accomplish their cooling effect with water, water solutions, or the coating effects of certain dry chemicals.

- Class B extinguishers diminish oxygen supplies and are used to suppress fires involving flammable liquids. A number of powdered chemicals, foam compounds, heavy non-combustible gases, and other agents are used in Class B extinguishers.
- Class C extinguishing agents are nonconductors and are used to combat electrical fires. Carbon dioxide (CO_2) is a common Class C fire extinguisher.
- Class D extinguishing agents are specially formulated to fight fires involving combustible metals and requiring a heat-absorbing extinguishing agent. Class D extinguishers contain various dry powders that will not react with the burning metal and may frequently be used in all other types of fires.

Selecting the proper extinguisher depends primarily on the hazards present at a particular facility; generally, a mix of types is appropriate. Extinguishers must be properly located and maintained. Security and safety departments should ensure that those responsible properly maintain all fire suppression equipment.

Before deciding which extinguishers to purchase, an in-depth survey of the facility must be made. The survey should give an accurate picture of the potential hazards of operation confronting each specific area and the facility as a whole. After extinguishers are selected, security personnel and other employees must be properly trained in their use.

Safety and security personnel should ensure compliance with applicable federal, state, and local laws and ordinances relating to fire suppression equipment in the workplace. Fire departments, zoning and building departments, fire marshals, and OSHA are excellent sources of additional information on industrial fire safety.

Sprinkler Protection

Portable fire extinguishers are transported to a fire location. Fixed or stationary fire extinguishing equipment is designed to control and extinguish a fire in a specific area. Fixed fire extinguishing systems utilize a variety of extinguishing agents, from water to chemical agents, depending on the application. They are automatic and discharge the extinguishing agent upon activation.

The most common type is the automatic water sprinkler system. Standard sprinkler installations usually consist of a combination of water sprinklers and one or more sources of water under pressure, water-flow controlling devices, distribution piping to supply the water to the discharge devices, alarms and supervisory devices, outdoor fire hydrants, indoor hose standpipes, and hand hose connections. The basic principles of water sprinkler protection evolve around the automatic discharge of water, in sufficient supply, to control or extinguish a fire in its initial stages.

The two primary types of automatic water sprinkler systems are the dry pipe and the wet pipe systems.

Wet Pipe Sprinkler

A wet pipe sprinkler system consists of automatic sprinklers attached to a system of piping that is actively charged with water under pressure. To avoid freezing, wet pipe systems are usually indoor systems. Sprinkler heads contain a fusible element that melts during a fire, releasing the water under pressure. As the water is released, the pressure changes, activating fire alarm sensors installed as an integral part of the system. The principal advantage of the wet pipe system is that, when activated, it will discharge water directly in the immediate area of the fire and at an early stage of the fire. Its primary disadvantage is that the fusible element contained in the sprinkler head must be melted before water is discharged and may cause a slight delay in detection and suppression.

Dry Pipe Sprinkler

Dry pipe sprinkler systems are charged with air under pressure and are used in exterior applications and other areas subject to freezing and areas presenting special hazards. The pressurized air is released by activation of a sensing device that opens a valve allowing pressurized water into the system to be discharged through the sprinklers, activating the fire alarm.

A routine program of inspection and maintenance of sprinkler systems should be developed. Security personnel are often given the responsibility of inspecting and ensuring that all components of the fire protection system are functional and in good working condition. Therefore, adequate training in the operation and care of sprinkler equipment should be given to security personnel.

Fire Protection Signals

Protective signaling devices play a major role in fire detection and protection and are used to:
- Notify people of a fire
- Call or alert the fire department and other professionals
- Monitor extinguishing systems and warn of activation, tampering and malfunctions
- Monitor industrial processes and warn of hazardous conditions
- Activate control and suppression equipment

The early stages of a fire are critical in detection, protection, containment, and suppression, thus making signaling devices an invaluable part of any fire safety system. Early detection can literally mean the difference between life and death. The presence and proper functioning of a protective signaling system is a major element in all safety and security programs.

Assorted types of detection and monitoring devices are utilized in protective signaling systems. As in the wet and dry piping systems, some monitor the water or air pressure of the system and activate when a sprinkler system, fire pump, or other fire protection device is activated or malfunctions. Some detect and react to fire conditions, heat, and smoke, with or without the activation of fire suppression equipment. As in all electronic safety and security equipment, fire alarm and detection technology changes frequently.

Workplace Fire Safety

The National Fire Safety Council and the National Fire Protection Association advise that fire losses exceed more than $2.2 billion annually and more than five thousand people are killed each year by fires in the United States. These organizations, along with the U.S. Department of Labor and Occupational Safety and Health Administration (OSHA), set standards and provide literature pertaining to workplace fire safety.

Workplace Safety

Federal, state, and local laws and the standards set by insurance carriers require employers to provide a safe and healthful work environment for employees. Again, OSHA is an excellent source of materials relating to workplace safety. Some jurisdictions have work safety regulations and environmental protection laws that are more stringent than those established by OSHA, and the federal government and insurance companies may set additional standards.

Accident Prevention

An effective accident prevention and occupational safety program in the workplace is a prime part of the security and safety operation. Safety is a term encompassing the areas of fire safety, personal security, and accident prevention. All employees must be initially trained and periodically retrained in general safety practices and in specific job-related responsibilities. Safety awareness, from the top of the management hierarchy to the lowest job classification, is imperative if safety hazards and violations are to be found, understood, and eliminated.

The security department, by its very nature, must play a major role in safety and accident prevention. Security personnel should be trained and knowledgeable of required safety standards and practices. The security professional is responsible for correcting or bringing about the correction of safety hazards and violations. Routine security duties—patrols, inspections, access control, etc.— expose security personnel to most, if not all, of the work environment, employees, operations, and potential safety problems and violations.

Summary

Fire is one of the most destructive forces known to man and can occur as an act of nature, as an accident, or as an act of sabotage. Regardless of its source, the potential for its occurrence can be reduced and resulting damage limited with an adequate fire prevention, protection, and suppression program. Training and practice, along with a basic knowledge of fire characteristics and fire suppression techniques and equipment can greatly reduce the fire threat.

The security department should provide support services to specialized fire protection personnel since fires and emergencies require both security and fire department services. Because they are often the first responders to a fire, security personnel should be deployed as part of an established plan that allows them to fulfill their responsibilities— assist in evacuations, control access and egress, facilitate the response of fire and police personnel, monitor alarm systems, etc. Safety is an important aspect of any environment and is a major responsibility of the security department. Legislation such as OSHA and workers' compensation laws has mandated that most work environments be safe and healthful places to work.

Chapter Eleven

Emergency and Disaster Control

If someone surveyed a small sampling of typical businesses, industries, or institutions to determine how they fared during emergency or disaster conditions, a wide range of responses would be collected. Some organizations are well prepared to safeguard the lives of their employees (and anyone else in their facilities), protect their physical plants, and often arrange to continue production (if only on a reduced basis) soon after a crisis.

Other organizations may not be as well prepared, but are able to continue functioning due to a unique product or service they provide, or due to their escaping the worst consequences of a disastrous situation.

However, the majority of American businesses, industries, and institutions suffer catastrophic losses every time a disaster strikes their organization. These different results are not necessarily due to differences in wealth, physical size, or number of employees, but rather are due to different degrees of emergency and disaster planning.

The Role of Planning

The only thing certain about planning to protect lives or property from natural or man-made emergencies or disasters is that there is no location, anywhere in the world, that is absolutely free from danger in one form or another. The varieties of potential dangers can be identified, however, and measures can be taken to reduce the risk of exposure to those dangers by people or property. Planning will not prevent a flood, an explosion, or a strike; however, thorough planning and preparation may prevent the escalation of a danger into catastrophe.

Unless the organization is small, high-ranking representatives should do the planning to cope with emergencies or disasters from all branches, departments, or sections, working together in a committee. The planning committee should not be too large, or agreements will be difficult to reach, but it should be large enough to ensure representation from all segments of the organization. Someone with knowledge of the security field, whether a staff member who has the responsibility for security or an outside security consultant, should be on the committee. However, the security manager should not be appointed as the committee head or sole investigator unless he holds a high position of authority in the organization. The following factors should be included in the planning process for an emergency and disaster control plan.
Authority

The owner, manager, or governing body of an organization should prepare a simple, written order to authorize the committee to develop the emergency control plan. The order should provide the committee with the necessary authority to develop a written plan and then organize, train, and assign responsibilities to an emergency force within the organization. This statement should be brief and flexible so that the committee can adjust its deliberations as necessary.

Existing organizational rules and regulations will have to be researched to ensure there is not already an emergency plan that has been overlooked or forgotten. A previous plan may or may not be adequate for the present situation, so it should be carefully reviewed and updated or declared void. Provisions for the new or revised emergency plan should follow the organization's established rules and regulations so that there is a formal, legal foundation for the emergency control program.

Written authority should exist to organize certain personnel into a special force during declared emergencies. There may be personnel occupying certain responsible positions who would object to such an extra assignment or who might be physically or emotionally unsuited for assignment to an emergency force. For this reason, an effort should be made to attract volunteers from the organization for the emergency force. Consideration for assignment to the force should be given to persons with unusual abilities and special interests that would be of benefit.

The personnel selected for the emergency force should undergo training in primary and alternate emergency duties. Cross-training the emergency force allows for a greater range of assignments and for the assumption of responsibilities in the event that another member is absent or becomes incapacitated.

Within larger organizations, there may be authority for personnel to be assigned as emergency coordinators for shifts, floors, buildings, or satellite facilities. This way, there will be trained personnel available throughout the organization to provide a continuity of calm leadership in an emergency.

The order of authority should also provide a chain of command that specifies the individuals who have the authority to order certain activities or changes or assume leadership roles in the event that higher-ranking personnel are unavailable during an emergency.

Vulnerability Assessment

Organizations that want to develop an emergency and disaster control plan must be aware of their existing vulnerabilities so that effective safeguards can be planned. A vulnerability assessment is performed in several phases. The first phase involves studying the frequency of the natural or man-made emergencies; the second concerns the physical plants; and the third assesses the present guard force.

A small committee should be appointed to conduct the vulnerability assessments. The first assessment merely identifies the types and frequencies of all natural and man-made emergencies and disasters recorded in the past in the area of the organization. If certain types of emergencies recur with regularity, predictions can be made as to the periods of the threats. Natural disasters seem to occur more regularly than man-made disasters.

The second phase of the vulnerability assessment requires an estimation of the structural strength of the buildings of the organization. An engineer should assist the committee in determining which of the buildings are sufficiently strong for use as shelters and which are structurally unsound and unsafe for use during natural disasters.

The third phase of the assessment should be an analysis of the organization's present security measures. The guards may be proprietary or contract, and their terms of employment may be such that they would not be available during periods of emergency. The employment of off-duty police officers is an example of this problem: They would be mobilized by the police department during a general emergency and would not be available to the private organization.

Another vulnerability assessment that should be made is the extent to which the organization would be affected by a disruption in electrical, water, sewerage, and communications services and the degree of isolation the facility would experience in event of flooded roadways, collapsed bridges, or other obstructions to normal transportation. The assessment should determine what alternate outside sources for these services would be readily available under disaster conditions and assess those supplies available from within the organization itself.

In those situations where the organization operates largely using outside cartage, supply, or labor under normal conditions, the capability of the vendors of those services should also be assessed to determine their ability to perform under emergency conditions.

Determining the Required Response or Security Needs

The vulnerability assessments should result in lists of vulnerable points in the physical structures and surrounding areas, the maintenance of power, communications and supplies, and sustained personnel support. Ultimately, the safeguarding of lives is of prime importance.

Therefore, the disaster plan developing committee should recommend to the facility administrator an order of priority of emergency responses to undertake under various threatening conditions. Questions such as when to order the evacuation of employees to in-house shelters or to other safe locations, whether any personnel should be exposed to danger by remaining in the insecure facility during the disaster, or when to order a shutdown of the production line must be resolved and instructions must be included in the disaster plan.

There must be a pre-established set of conditions and instructions prepared to cover any emergency. There should be limited personal discretion allowed for personnel involved in emergency operations.

Appointment of the Emergency and Disaster Control Coordinator

Large organizations may have the resources to appoint a full-time emergency or disaster control coordinator to manage the rest of the development or implementation of the plan. In smaller organizations, someone may have to assume this role part-time. In any event, the coordinator should be of sufficient stature and authority in the organization that he would be able to deal effectively with others at all levels in the organizational hierarchy. Not only must he understand the value of preparedness, but he also must engender support for the program in periods when emergencies and disasters appear to be no threat. In all cases, he must ensure that every facet of the plan be cost-effective.

The appointment of the coordinator does not mean the end of the original committee' s responsibilities in further developing the disaster plan. Rather, the appointment will be another sign from top management that there will be support for this project. The continued active use of this committee will also help in gaining support from the separate departments, which the members of the committee represent.

Gaining Management Support

The next step in the planning process is to acquaint management of all levels with the vulnerabilities of the organization to emergencies or disasters and to solicit their advice and cooperation for the development of a disaster control program. The support of management is necessary because there will need to be financial expenditures, personnel use, and the possible acquisition or sharing of equipment.

Use of In-House Personnel

Regardless of the size of the organization, the presently employed personnel should perform the majority, if not all, of the necessary emergency duties.

The nucleus of the emergency organization can be those personnel already trained and utilized to perform routine and emergency services, such as the foremen, supervisors, and other key administrative personnel, as well as the existing medical, fire, safety, and security staff. Other emergency response personnel can be selected from the regular employees who have demonstrated special talents or interests that could be useful, such as CB or ham radio operators, volunteer or auxiliary police or firemen, first aid instructors, or recreational vehicle operators (boats, snowmobiles, aircraft).

The regular maintenance or engineering employees could help to survey, establish, and maintain emergency facilities and make damage assessments. Personnel administrators could be responsible for the shelter and welfare services in the facility. Any research or scientifically oriented personnel could be used to monitor radiological sensors or other essential equipment or communications. As the emergency preparedness plan develops, other employees may be found to have special skills or an interest in training to acquire additional skills that would contribute to the response effort.

Sources of Assistance

Planning must also incorporate as much self-help as possible during such emergencies to minimize the cost to the organization.

Self-Help

An important aspect of the vulnerability assessment is to identify the activities and material that are presently located within the surveyed facility. Not only must the regular employees be selected and trained for their responsive roles, but any material or supplies, such as food, water, tools, portable equipment, lumber, or other property that could be used to protect or repair the facility or to recover from interrupted services, must be in inventories and kept in usable condition.

The vulnerability assessment should also estimate the amount of emergency supplies (sandbags, plywood, nails, etc.) that would be necessary in the event that a certain building or facility had to be protected or occupied throughout an emergency. Many organizations will have within their facilities supplies that could be utilized as makeshift material to block doors and windows, provide a limited water supply, or serve as emergency rations.

In cases of large organizations that are widely dispersed geographically, the assessment might identify such necessary items that would be available within the organization and the effort that would be required to shift those items to wherever they are most needed. Such organizational managers then would request purchasing extra material and equipment that would be of use only during an emergency.

Mutual Aid Agreements

It is well known that people help each other during emergencies. What is necessary to benefit the most from this trait is to plan ahead for those emergencies that are most likely to occur and thereby maximize the chances that help will be available from and to others as needed.

A mutual aid agreement may involve either distant facilities of one organization, similar organizations, all businesses or activities within a neighborhood, or governmental agencies. There are advantages and disadvantages in the use of mutual aid agreements, so the committee doing the planning will have to explore all possible assistance, select the most advantageous, and maintain open communications for changing to more appropriate sources if necessary.

As mentioned in the section concerning the use of in-house personnel during emergencies or disasters, whenever there is an emergency, certain personnel (National Guard personnel, firemen, policemen) may have a legal obligation to report elsewhere, and so will be unavailable for emergency or disaster assignments within the organization.

When in-house personnel are unavailable and manpower is needed, another organization might have a list of volunteers who would agree to assist the requesting firm. There should be no high expectations that temporary employees can be hired through normal employment agencies during emergencies, because those personnel are less likely to have a sense of loyalty or trust that would be needed in an emergency.

Naturally, supplies, equipment, special clothing, food, and some financial remuneration must be made available to any outside personnel, just as would be done for in-house employees working beyond normal periods. The legal liabilities for damages, injuries, and deaths caused by both in-house and mutual aid agreement personnel must be established during this planning stage.

When some supplies, material, or equipment are not available within the organization, a mutual agreement with the nearest facility that has such items may be warranted. However, it must always be considered that whenever one facility is in need of such items, the same items may also be needed by the facility that possesses them. Another factor to be considered is that when there is a dire need for certain property that is in scarce supply, the price may become high, if not exorbitant. For these reasons, alternate sources should be identified locally, as well as from facilities that are some distance away from the affected area.

There are some mutual aid agreements between private firms and governmental agencies, such as fire or police departments. In such agreements, private firefighting equipment and personnel are pledged to stand by whenever the public firefighters are called out. Private security personnel are also afforded limited police powers when they are deputized or are provided such limited powers by local ordinance for special occurrences. In such cases, the mutual aid agreements are limited because the police and fire departments may have stronger mutual aid pacts with other governmental agencies that would take precedence.

Government and Public Services

It may be surprising, but even organizations that prepare emergency plans often do not take advantage of available government information on the subject. The emergency planning committee should contact the various government agencies that can provide this assistance.

The Federal Emergency Management Agency (2400 M Street NW, Washington, D.C. 20472) provides published information and recommendations on how to counteract and minimize losses caused by enemy action, natural, or man-made disasters. That office should be contacted for an up-to-date bibliography of related U.S. Government Printing Office publications.

Regional emergency and disaster agencies can provide additional information that may have a more local orientation concerning emergencies that are most likely to occur. As the local coordinating agency for emergency and disaster situations, they can also provide recommendations for local responses to ensure the fullest cooperation and protective measures appropriate to the area.

State and local governments provide police, fire, and other services, including environmental protection, health and welfare, and many more services during normal periods as well as during emergency conditions.

Public and public service agencies may provide water, electricity, telephone communications, sanitation, and other services. These agencies should be contacted to learn how they plan to continue their services during an emergency.

Not every police, fire department, or other agency will be able to provide the exact services nationwide. For that reason, it is the planning committee's responsibility to establish exactly what services would be available during various emergency situations and acquire information on how alternative services can be obtained.

One problem seldom considered in emergency planning is the identification of employees with unusual health or disability impairments. There are many people in the general population who can function only with constant medical attention, medication, or clinical services. Those persons handicapped by severe color or night blindness, diabetes, or epilepsy, for instance, may not only be unable to contribute to emergency functions, but may require special help and attention themselves during the emergency.

Therefore, such people should provide instructions as to how they might be helped (name and phone number of physician, medication source, etc.) in the event their malady is aggravated during an emergency.

The vulnerability surveys should have determined the areas with a need for additional personnel support during emergencies. There are several ways to increase personnel strengths from within the organization. One way is to eliminate or decrease non-critical activities and reassign those personnel temporarily. Another way would be to reduce administrative staffs by deferring or postponing non-essential duties until after the emergency subsides. A third way would be to solicit spouses and relatives of present employees to either contribute their services or to accept temporary employment.

The employment of additional personnel from among people with a vested interest in the organization may be more productive and involve less risk than hiring outsiders who would have no loyalty for the organization.

Developing the Plan

The existing organizational structure, already familiar to the employees, should be utilized as much as practicable when developing the emergency plan. The regular supervisory authority, technical skills, equipment and material on hand should form the foundation for emergency plans and actions. In this respect, the disaster organization will not be seen as a strange or separate entity, and possibly as a threat, by the remainder of the organization. The following factors should be considered in the development of the disaster plan:

- The conditions requiring the activation of the emergency or disaster control program should be listed.
- The person or persons with the authority to declare an emergency should be identified.
- Maps and blueprints of the facility to be protected should be provided.

- An emergency control center and an alternate site should be designated.
- Communications facilities between the control center, the major sections of the facility, and the community should be established. Alternate means of communication (radios, sound-powered phones, etc.) should be provided.
- An emergency organization hierarchy should be developed, and a list of employees and their emergency duties should be available.
- Emergency shutdown procedures should be developed, and lists made of critical property and records to be secured.
- Emergency evacuations should be planned.
- Shelters should be identified and supplied with food, medical supplies, water, and disaster equipment.
- An augmented security force should be planned.
- Damage assessment and repair teams should be designated.
- Emergency power, fuel, and utilities should be ready to be activated as needed.
- Plans for cooperation with federal, state, and local police, fire, and emergency preparedness officials should be developed. Mutual aid pacts should be set up.
- Records should be kept of all activities that take place during the emergency for satisfaction of legal liabilities and possible later revision of the disaster plan.

A sound emergency and disaster control plan is the result of thorough advance planning, testing, revision, and updating. An adequate emergency plan must contain detailed and timely information about the resources that can be utilized in the most efficient and expeditious manner.

The plan for emergency control must consider the goals, products, and personnel within the facility. Goal changes, shifting responsibilities, and personnel turnover may require the frequent updating of the basic plan. Therefore, emergency planning must be an ongoing process if the best safeguards possible are expected.

All planned emergency control measures must be arranged so that they complement and supplement each other, the regular security force, and the primary goals of the parent organization. Poorly integrated emergency control measures may result in the waste of manpower, funds, and equipment. Of greater importance, the lack of integration in the plans may jeopardize the safety and security of the facility.

The Role of Security

Security forces have a crucial role during emergency operations. There has been little reference to the regular security forces up to this point, because emergency or disaster planning for any type of organization entails the orderly and efficient transition from normal to emergency operations by the regular workforce. The energy and power of the regular workforce is many times greater than the security personnel could provide. Still, the role of security is crucial in that a greater degree of protection must be provided in a period of crisis.

The size of the security force available to an organization during an emergency is usually the same as under normal conditions. There are few proprietary or contract guard services that have large numbers of reserve personnel who wait for an emergency or disaster to happen.

Because of the limited numbers of guards that are available to a firm, their roles usually do not differ greatly during normal and emergency operating conditions. Yet because of the aura of authority associated with the guards, most people expect them to be thoroughly trained in every aspect of the emergency operation.

This means that the guard forces should know and understand every aspect of the emergency or disaster program, even though their role remains security-oriented. During the emergency, they should be kept abreast of programs of the operation so that they can be a source of information for other employees.

Security personnel have the ultimate responsibility for ensuring that only authorized personnel are admitted to the facility, that restricted zones are for limited personnel only, and that personnel entering and leaving the plant should be properly accounted for. The logging of employees and visitors in and out of the facility may seem unnecessary, but during emergencies, the log may be of inestimable value in locating persons, in identifying those in certain areas, and possibly for the identification of bodies.

The guards should be trained to perform guard duties during emergencies. They may be given cross training with fire personnel in order to augment their forces or to learn how fire or safety personnel perform rescue operations. But it must be remembered that rescue operations are best conducted by those forces who are provided with specialized equipment, training, and in-depth knowledge of the unseen dangers of the facility, such as high-voltage power lines, deadly fumes, or dangers of explosion.

The guard service must be organized in such a way that they can be deployed to protect the areas of high vulnerability. Temporary measures to secure areas from intrusion by the use of barbed wire, vehicle emplacement, trespass signs, and various alarm systems should be considered.

Another important point is to ensure the availability of guard personnel and transportation to respond promptly to calls for assistance. When the facility remains in full or partial operation during the emergency, there are certain areas that will need extra guard help to facilitate the movement and control of employees, such as gates and parking lots.

During an emergency, security duties will increase beyond the capability of the available personnel, so plans should be made for the augmenting of the security force with persons selected from the regular workforce. There may be employees with previous police or military experience who would require little training or supervision to provide support services to the guards. When provided with a special armband or stenciled hardhat, they might be employed at gates to check identification or as the second member of a guard patrol.

Finally, the question arises about arming the guards. Many guard forces are not armed. Some have arms available to them via their guard supervisors or in arms lockers. Others are armed at all times. The value of equipment or merchandise, the danger to life or property, recent criminal attacks in the area, and other factors will dictate the armaments necessary. The emergency and disaster control plan committee should resolve that question in consultation with the organization's legal officer, the police, and the prosecutor's office.

Training for Emergencies

The objective of a training program is to ensure that all emergency force personnel are able to perform their special duties quickly and efficiently. The extent and type of training required to properly prepare emergency control forces will vary according to the importance, vulnerability, size, and other unique factors affecting the particular facility.

Thorough and continuing training is the most effective means to obtain and maintain the maximum proficiency of the emergency force personnel. Regardless of how carefully emergency personnel are selected; it is seldom that they will initially have all the qualifications and experience to be effective team members without cooperative training. Furthermore, new and revised emergency requirements frequently mean that personnel must be retrained. Training can bridge the gap between the job requirement and personal ability.

Thorough training has many benefits for both the organization and the emergency control program. Supervisors realize benefits because the trained personnel are easier to supervise; there is less wasted time; and fewer mistakes are made. The resultant economies are of benefit to the organization. The confidence that is instilled by training affects the morale and welfare of the entire organization.

The individual emergency personnel also benefit from training through increased knowledge and skills, increased opportunities for personal advancement, and a better understanding of their relationship to the emergency program and the parent organization.

Testing the Plan

When the disaster plan has been completed, provisions for its implementation and testing must be made. This is the time when deficiencies and unrealistic features of the plan are discovered and corrected.

The main goals of such a test include the following:

- To familiarize all personnel in the emergency force with the overall plan and to acquaint each person with his own emergency duties and responsibilities
- To evaluate the workability of the plan and identify deficiencies
- To make the necessary adjustments to the plan for future testing and implementation

There are different ways to test an emergency disaster control plan. The most comprehensive method would be to test the plan in three phases. The first phase would be to test the key individuals separately. Then the plan would be tested in each section or department within the facility. The third phase would be a test of the response of the entire facility. Various conditions could be simulated for each phase, or if one threat is considered more likely than the others are, one type of emergency could be simulated for all three phases.

After the emergency control coordinator and the planning committee are satisfied that they have a workable plan, they might coordinate further testing with local emergency preparedness exercises to determine the plan's compatibility with the local effort.

There is no hard and fast rule as to how often an emergency plan should be tested. There must be a continuing and concerted effort to upgrade the response capabilities of the personnel selected for the emergency operation. In order to keep personnel familiar with the plan and to familiarize new personnel with their responsibilities, further individual, departmental, and facility testing should be conducted as needed, at least annually and possibly semiannually.

Chapter Twelve

The Security Survey

This is the "bread and butter" of the security consulting practice. The security survey is a tool for you, the consultant, and a report for the client. You can' t fix what you don't understand. The survey is your method of auditing, evaluating, examining, investigating, and reviewing the facilities, functions, personnel, and all other facets of the security program. At the end of this chapter are three real-life samples of security surveys. Everything you have learned, to this point, was designed to assist in the gathering of the information needed to successfully complete a professional security survey.

Your survey can be used to improve existing systems, evaluate operations, or determine requirements and develop a totally new security program. Security surveys and threat assessments are made to determine the degree of exposure to hazards or dangers to personnel and property

Outside consultants are free of organizational ties that tend to diminish objectivity. The consultant may observe threatening factors that have been accepted as normal conditions or something that cannot be changed by an internal security employee. Because the consultant has limited knowledge of the subject of the consult, he or she must be thoroughly diligent in observing everything within the domain of the survey.

Frequently, large organizations with full-time security directors tend to be reluctant to admit the need of assistance from outside, regardless of how limited in experience their own personnel are. They sometimes consider the security consultant as a threat to their position and influence. The professional consultant will quickly attempt to defuse this situation and reinforce the belief that the results of the consultant's work will benefit the security department.

Some small organizations assume they cannot afford to hire outside consultants and believe they can obtain security advice from their insurance agents or local police. Many organizations are wary that an outside consultant is primarily interested in the sale of security hardware, regardless of its need; therefore, it is imperative that security consultants be separate from sales personnel and maintain objectivity at all times.

A professional security survey or threat assessment can only be accomplished when there is complete organizational support by both management and operational personnel. Management must provide the authority, autonomy, and financial support necessary for the survey. Operational personnel must be supportive of management's efforts to improve safety and security in the workplace.

Threat Assessment

The purpose of a security survey and threat assessment is to determine the vulnerability of a specific organization, facility, or activity to the hazards and dangers caused by natural and man-made forces. The consultant develops a survey plan based on affording total security to the organization, facility, or personnel being serviced, while recognizing that total security may not be cost-effective or supported by senior management. Priorities must be established that enable all items to receive security appropriate to their value

The first step in a security survey is to ascertain the value, impact, or cost of any asset should it be lost to the client. The consultant will need to obtain the identification and relative value of the buildings, equipment, and activities in the area to be surveyed and how important they are to continued productivity for the entire organization. Some equipment, for example, may have relatively low purchase value but contain highly classified proprietary information. In this case, the information gets the priority rather than the equipment itself. Priorities for protection should be assigned to the areas most critical to the survival and success of the organization, while non-critical areas should be assigned a lesser priority for protection.

The security consultant needs to gain the cooperation of the operating personnel in order to discover the actual processes followed throughout a normal period of operation. As the consultant verifies the actual procedures undertaken by operating personnel, he can then apply the appropriate priorities of protection. After the facility has been inspected and the priorities assigned, conduct of the formal survey can begin.

Situations sometimes arise in which management or operational personnel disagree with the priorities established by the consultant. To avoid such opposition, the consultant should consider forming a three-person quality process team with representation by knowledgeable management and employee personnel and the consultant. Each team member assigns his own priorities and then discusses them with the other members. Objective and valid priorities are usually attained by averaging the priority scores.

The next stage of a security survey and threat assessment is to determine the vulnerability of the facility or activity. Buildings with large numbers of openings to the outside (doors, windows, skylights, etc.) are the objects of more man-made attacks than buildings with fewer openings. Hard targets, buildings with fences, lights, guards, and alarm systems are victimized less frequently than facilities without such protection. The amount of criminal activity in the surrounding area should also be examined, as it is likely to have a direct bearing on attacks against the facility and to persons arriving or departing from the facility.

Vulnerability risk is also in proportion to the value of items contained in the facility. Cash and small, high-value items like jewelry, cameras, and drugs are more frequently the target of theft than are large and heavy material with little resale value.

Natural forces also have an impact on the vulnerability of a facility. The building codes of most jurisdictions address construction concerns as they pertain to specific natural disaster problems. For example, buildings in Florida must meet certain specifications relating to protection against hurricanes, while buildings in California must be constructed in such a manner to withstand earthquakes of a certain magnitude. Local records should be reviewed to determine the frequency and severity of earthquakes, floods, or other disastrous natural forces. Engineers and government experts (federal, state, and local) can provide assistance in determining regional vulnerability to natural disaster. Loss due to theft and looting increases after natural disasters and must be taken into account as well.

To determine vulnerability, the security consultant should examine the facility at least twice. The facility should be observed both during peak operational periods and during closed or slack times. Nighttime visits are important, even if the facility is non-operational. The consultant should inspect the facilities to determine current security and to discover weak points. Weaknesses in the security program—poor lighting, missing or damaged security hardware, inattentive guards, etc.— will increase the vulnerability of the facility.

High or increasing rates of loss should alert the consultant to a vulnerability problem. The record of losses, if any are kept, may give insight to vulnerability. The records should be examined analytically to look for the answers as to who, what, when, where, how, and why. The security consultant will find that records of loss are frequently nonexistent or poorly maintained. If this is the case, recommendations for correction should be included in your final report. Out of fear of reprimand, many losses go unreported to higher management. Some businesses fail to report losses to avoid increases in their insurance premiums. When records don' t exist, the consultant will have to get such information from the employees through routine interviews.

Vulnerability may be further determined by examining whether high-value property is properly protected from theft by insiders. Frequently, the location for storage of high-risk items is chosen without considering the problem of internal theft and may be near exits, restrooms, or trash bins. High-risk items located there should be relocated to a less traveled or open area.

Retail stores most frequently locate the cashier's office, camera department, and other high-risk areas some distance away from outside doors. The knowledge that a long route must be traversed in order to escape does have an effect upon the number of transgressions occurring deep within the store.

As the survey is conducted, a chart can be prepared that will illustrate the degree of vulnerability of the various areas.

The third criterion applicable to a risk assessment is the degree of probability that natural or man-made forces will strike any given organization, facility, or activity. There is a high probability of disastrous storms along the hurricane belt. Blizzards are commonplace in the North and Midwest. Low-lying valleys with rivers or valleys below dams stand a high chance of flash floods during rainy seasons. Earthquakes occur with regularity in the West, and even volcanoes erupt. The degree of probability of such occurrences can be estimated with fair success when based upon past experiences. Attacks by man can likewise be predicted after all the high priority and vulnerability factors have been considered.

Generally, one can observe the rate of past experiences of natural or man-made forces and determine whether there is an increase, decrease, or relatively constant number of events occurring over a period of time. When coupled with such factors as high priority for security, a high vulnerability risk, and frequent devastating storms, the probability of loss is high. The lack or infrequency of natural disasters, the absence of physical losses, and low impact in event of loss would predict a lower or insignificant loss probability.

The loss probability can likewise be estimated for attacks by man. A chart can be prepared to show the number of known depredations committed for various periods in the past. There is some value to reviewing the loss records for as long ago as ten or more years. Such a review might disclose a favorable or unfavorable record of security, but more importantly, the record allows a comparison with the rate of criminal activity during the past year. Increasing or decreasing trends in crime can be determined and may provide top management with the data that will support a request for a stronger security policy or additional funding.

Designing Security Surveys

The type of security survey to be conducted of any organization, facility, or activity is dictated by the purpose of the survey and by the kind of facility to be surveyed. As stated earlier, surveys can be conducted to determine the relative risks of losses from natural and man-made forces, but not all the information gathered by one type of survey will be of help in recommending protective services for the other. Therefore, most surveys will have to be carefully designed to incorporate the specific goals and the unique physical and personnel structure of each organization.

Surveys generally specify one or more of the following listed objectives:

- Determine the existent vulnerabilities to injury, death, damage or destruction by natural causes
- Determine the existent vulnerabilities of corporate assets due to criminal activity from outside the organization
- Determine the existent vulnerabilities of corporate assets due to criminal activity from within the organization
- Determine the existent conditions of physical security of corporate property
- Measure the effectiveness of the current protection policies and standards
- Measure the conformity of the employees to the published security standards
- Audit the accounts and procedures of the firm to detect policy violations, fraud, and use of improper procedures
- Inspect the conditions and procedures that cause the problems of inventory shortages, cash or property losses, vandalism, or other unexplained crime within the plant
- Investigate the economic-sociological-political conditions in the community to predict outside activities that could be adverse to the well being or survival of the company

A cursory glance at these objectives will reveal that the requested surveys may be instigated as a reaction to recurring problems within the organization, or simply as a result of a regularly scheduled program to assess conditions before they become risks or losses.

In practice, there are some security agencies that make a distinction between physical security surveys and crime prevention surveys. The rationale given is that although physical security measures do prevent crime, they are oriented more toward the security of property and facilities, whereas crime prevention measures encompass the deterrence of criminal activity regardless of the extent or availability of physical safeguards.

One operative definition of physical security is "that part of security concerned with the physical measures designed to safeguard personnel, to prevent unauthorized access to equipment, facilities, material and documents, and to safeguard them against espionage, sabotage, damage and theft." The physical measures cited in the definition are those concerning perimeter security, lighting, locks, intrusion detection systems, storage containers, and security personnel. In other terms, a physical security survey is directed toward a detailed examination and to specific recommendations provided for the application of physical measures to prevent the opportunity to commit a crime.

Despite the proliferation of survey checklists throughout the security industry, few of them are totally compatible with all the survey objectives or are applicable to all facilities. Yet they do provide a guideline to the surveyor so that the most obvious conditions are not overlooked.

There are advantages and disadvantages to the use of checklists. They do serve as a reminder that specific subjects or areas should be inspected. Checklists can be devised and used as an outlined draft of the final report. The checklists can direct the examination of the facility from the exterior to the interior, or from the general to the specific features that must be observed and reported. The use of a checklist can also help other surveyors to continue the survey should the initial surveyor have to leave the assignment.

On the other hand, many surveyors do no more than what is prescribed by the checklist, thereby limiting their own contribution. The checklist may have been adapted from another facility or agency and not be totally applicable to the surveyed facility. Surveyors can become accustomed to checking off items rather than describing the situation by their own terminology, which may be more precise. Finally, checklists tend to allow the surveyors to make a more cursory inspection, whereas the narrative report would require a more detailed examination to properly describe the item reported.

There are no hard and fast rules on how to conduct a survey. Some have been performed as a hasty walk-through with a single-page checklist, while others involve lengthy preparation and visits for several weeks. The more experienced consultant may be able to complete a survey in a fraction of the time it would take a novice. In any case, following an organized design of survey activities is recommended in addition to obtaining specific instructions from the client.

Preliminary Activities

Written authority to conduct the survey should be obtained. This authority should clearly outline the goals and objectives of the survey and establish time, support, and availability of other administrative facilities for the use of the surveyor.

The historical, geographical, and other background data of the facility and its environs should be reviewed. The local media and public records should be checked in order to establish the relationships and attitudes of the facility and the local community. Local crime rates should be compared with the rate of crime occurring in the facility.

A review of the written policies, rules, regulations, and standard operating procedures or other instructions relating to security should be made.

Maps, floor plans, or architectural drawings should be obtained to determine the main characteristics, especially the locations of doors and windows.

A review of any previous surveys that have been reported should be made.

A checklist containing questions that must be answered to satisfy the initial purpose of the survey should be assembled.

Performing the Survey

The survey should review, with the management personnel and supervisors of the organization, the facilities or activities to be surveyed and the purposes of the survey. This review should engender their cooperation and solicit their continued contribution to the survey.

An orientation tour should be made to establish the limits of the facility. The area supervisors should be solicited for their concept of the corporate security policy and standards. They should also demonstrate all security procedures applicable to their area of jurisdiction. Arrangements should be made to review these procedures with supervisors on all shifts.

The facility should be visited during peak and low operating periods to personally observe the personnel, procedures, and physical measures, including the perimeter barriers, the lighting, locking devices, intrusion detection systems, storage containers, and the security personnel.

The survey checklist should be expanded wherever there is a need to do so. Further, narrative descriptions of any features of the security program should be recorded if necessary. Photographs should be taken of objects or situations that are difficult to describe.

Coordinating Interviews

There should be a review with the local supervisors of all the deficiencies that were noted so that immediate corrective action can be taken. In some security programs, the local supervisors must prepare a written list of corrective actions taken shortly after this review.

On occasion, the local supervisors will quarrel with the survey findings. For this reason and for the sake of fairness, the surveyor must be careful to point out only genuine deficiencies in security, and not employ harassing tactics or exaggerate in order to emphasize his own importance.

The Survey Report

Survey reports must follow the requirements of the requestor. Some reports are merely cover letters attached to the checklists. It may be true that the requestor need not be provided with details beyond a brief list of deficiencies and recommendations. The extent of the details of the survey report should be prescribed by the original request.

Survey reports may spell out a complete narrative description of the physical plant and the prescribed security policies or standards so that the reader may make a direct comparison of the report with the facility surveyed.

When there is a notation in the report that there is a deficiency because an existent security measure does not meet the organizational standard, it would be redundant to add that the deficiency should be removed, but recommendations should be fully described.

The Follow-Up Survey

A follow-up is performed to ensure that the deficiencies have been corrected or are actively and consistently repaired.

It should be scheduled after a sufficient period of time has passed in which corrective actions can be taken to eliminate the deficiencies. This period may be thirty, sixty, or ninety days. Any period longer than that may leave security risks uncorrected for too long a time. The follow-up survey reviews only those areas with deficiencies.

Any evidence that the deficiencies and recommendations have been ignored must be taken to the top management level of the organization.

Frequency of Surveys

There are no strict rules that prescribe how often surveys should be conducted in a specific facility. Corporate-level security policy should provide some flexible guidelines for the security surveyor to follow. The following listed conditions may help to determine the appropriate frequency of surveys.

In the case of a new organization, facility, or activity, a thorough survey should be made to ensure that there is a complete record of the security measures and any security deficiencies. The frequency of subsequent surveys should consider the extent of the risks of vulnerability, priority (criticality), and probability. If the facility is in a high-risk category and depredations against corporate property are constant, surveys should be scheduled at greater frequencies, perhaps as often as quarterly or semiannually. When the facility appears to have a low risk rating, annual surveys should be considered.

One method to provide the impression that security has a high priority is to conduct inspections of units of the larger organization throughout the year after the initial survey. In this manner, smaller inspections or audits of the physical security measures or of operating procedures, alternated throughout the organization, may provide a habit of security consciousness among employees. The conduct of organization-wide surveys would not need to be more frequently than annually. The smaller units inspected may be selected on a rotational or random basis, or they may be selected based upon the number of security problems that surface after the initial survey.

Frequency of security surveys may also be increased after serious or repeated depredations against the firm. However, the actual point of attack may not be the weak link in security, so any investigation of the security problems should extend beyond the obvious scene. In the case of repeated attacks, the survey frequently should be increased until a way has been found to solve or reduce the problem.

New surveys should be considered every time the facility reorganizes its physical structures or personnel, or after the acquisition of new buildings or expensive equipment. The risk probability, vulnerabilities, and security priorities will no doubt change under those conditions. Extensive changes of property or equipment indicate a need for all-inclusive surveys, but minor changes or mere additions of new equipment in already high-security areas may need only a less inclusive update survey.

These suggestions do not include every reason why a new or additional survey should be made. It is the responsibility of the security supervisors and top management to promptly evaluate any change that may increase risk to the organization's well being or survival.

Cost-Benefit Analysis

Not all commercial or industrial firms or institutions have regularly organized security plans, programs, or security personnel. About 58 percent of the ten million businesses in this country gross less than

$100,000 annually. Taken together, these smaller firms suffer larger losses from criminal action and employ a disproportionately smaller number of security measures to protect their assets. Additionally, the smaller firms suffer a higher rate of bankruptcies, and not a few of the bankruptcies are caused by shoplifting and employee theft. Small business owners complain that they cannot afford security, but in reality they cannot afford not to have security.

At first glance, an outsider might conjecture that security personnel are only window dressing and do not contribute productively to business firms. That line of reasoning is fallacious at best. Even in the old days, when every factory had its own guard to watch the building for security purposes, the guards were additionally productive by their oiling machinery, emptying trashcans, and providing other non-security services. They may have earned more of their pay by their other services, unless they were lucky enough to prevent a fire, thwart a burglary, or perform some life-saving act for an employee. But those kinds of events were rare and are still relatively rare today.

The most difficult task of the modern security manager is to justify the expenses of security. The security program is still largely seen as a group of little old men making certain the coffee pots are unplugged and that some worker has not thrown a smoldering cigarette butt into a paper-filled trash can.

The security manager can change that old image of the security department by preparing a cost-benefit analysis for his unit. A cost-benefit analysis is a direct comparison of the costs of the operation of the security unit and all security measures with the amount of corporate property saved or recovered and elimination or reduction of losses caused by injuries and lost production time. Despite the claim that it is impossible to compute the savings incurred through crime prevented by the security officer's presence, there are methods for computing the relative values of security measures.

The first rule of a cost-benefit accounting system is to not recommend a security measure that is not cost-effective. That is to say that one should not spend $10,000 to protect a $5 object. Nor should one erect a $10,000 fence to secure a junk car worth $100. But a $10,000 fence would be cost-effective if it were built to protect something valued several times greater than the fence.

Extending that idea, the security manager should be able to show over a period of time that the services of his department at a cost of X dollars have effectively decreased losses from X dollars in year so-and-so to Z dollars this past year. In other instances, the security manager may be able to show that although the remainder of the community had a crime rate increase, his jurisdiction actually had a decrease.

Although a direct dollar loss or gain cannot always be seen in such a direct comparison, some evaluations may be estimated for illustration purposes.

Every structure and its contents have a dollar value assigned by the organization. Estimates of the cost of fire, vandalism, or theft can be made and projected showing the probability rate of occurrence if security is not effective.

Estimates of lost time due to theft of equipment or materials would likewise present a good argument that security is cost-effective in its preventive measures.

There are often some reductions in insurance premium rates if alarm systems, fire sprinklers, or guards are employed, which contributes to a cost saving.

If the security personnel become more adept at their job and actually improve their apprehension and recovery rate, the total values of the property saved and recovered and decreased expenses may show a surprisingly satisfactory cost-benefit relationship.

Ultimately, the security manager may investigate the possibility of replacing some of the security personnel with electronic devices that would cost a fraction of the guard's annual salary. Not only would the operating budget be lowered by such mechanisms, but also management may become so appreciative with the cost-benefit results that the money saved through the listed methods might be returned to the security unit's budget as an increase the following year.

Selling the Security Plan

There is no single method for selling a security plan to management. The best way to sell a security plan is to apply some basic logical principles to the preparation of the security plan so that management will readily recognize that the proper work has been done.

The transitional steps in planning should be followed when a security measure is proposed:

- Recognize a need
- State the objectives
- Gather the relevant data
- Develop alternatives
- Prepare a course of action
- Analyze the capabilities
- Review the plan
- Present the plan to management

The presentation should be made with consideration of the organization's financial situation at the time of the proposal. If the firm is cutting back its budget, any savings suggested by the plan should be highlighted. If the organization is in an expansion phase, the presentation should emphasize how the proposal fits into such a plan. The security manager should be able to dovetail any proposal into the firm's present plans; otherwise, there may be a summary rejection because the plan is out of step.

Most proposals for changes or additions to programs must be presented to management in such a fashion as will favorably attract their attention. Clean, well-prepared reports, audio-visual aids, large charts, etc. will serve to get across the message that effort was expended to present this case. Nothing should be left to chance. The more that is known about the plan that is to be sold to management, the greater will be the confidence of the presenter. And the greater his confidence, the easier it will be to convince management that this plan will work. There is no guarantee, of course, that management will adopt proposals, but following these steps will provide for a better presentation.

Maintaining Corporate Support

After the new security plan has been sold to management, the security manager will have the responsibility for implementing the plan and maintaining management's continued support for it. Without both moral and financial support, most programs seldom last for very long.

One of the most effective ways for the security director to maintain the interest and support of management is to become a more involved member of management. There are many ways he can become more active and accepted, including the ready acceptance of added responsibilities, the participation in the less popular programs, and an attitude and demeanor that will set an example of honesty, seriousness, and dependability.

The security director, by virtue of his position, must be the leader, not only in his own specialty, but also among other activities of the organization. Volunteering to assist in fund drives, setting the example by quickly responding to those in need, and constantly serving selflessly will engender respect and support from all levels of personnel. In that respect, management would be hard-pressed not to support their most proficient manager.

Chapter Thirteen

Sample Security Surveys

SAMPLE SECURITY SURVEY – <mark>NARRATIVE FORMAT</mark>:

Utilizing this format, the consultant prepares the report in narrative from directly from his observations.

ABC Company Security Survey

OLS1JOO1 (unique ID#)

The number presented here represents the unique numbers provided for site specific locations based on a CAP ® Index, Threat Assessment Report. The consultant can devise his/her own unique numbering system.

For:

(Your Client)
Corporate Center
Anytown, USA 12345

September 10, 1999

Your Security Services Company, Inc.
Senior Consultant

Contents

Points of Contact & Building Data

Executive Summary

Office Building Information

Warehouse Building Information

Security and Lighting

Requirements and Justifications

Recommendations

Attachments

A – Threat Analysis Site Data

B – CAP ® Index Report and Map

C – Security Incident Reports

D – 1999 Police Department Calls

E – Fire & Life Safety Guide

F – Lighting Survey Site Plans

Points of Contact & Building Data

Building Locations: Corporate Center
Anytown, USA 12345

Building Management: ABC Company

Building Manager & Telephone: John Doe (555) 555-5555

Survey Contact Jane Doe

Lead Technician Jack Doe (555) 555-5555

Additional identifying data as may be needed.

Office Buildings Surveyed (the physical descriptions and layouts)

Five- floor professional office building (278,456 sq. ft.)
Five-floor professional office building (130,692 sq. ft.)
Six -floor professional office building (186,421 sq. ft.)
Five-floor professional office building (120,743 sq. ft.)
Five-floor professional office building (106,806 sq. ft.)
Five-floor professional office building (121,205 sq. ft.)

Warehouses Surveyed (descriptive data)

Multi-tenant warehouse (119,650 sq. ft.)
Multi-tenant warehouse (151,705 sq. ft.)
Multi-tenant warehouse (130,752 sq. ft.)
Multi-tenant warehouse (115,095 sq. ft.)
Multi-tenant warehouse (142,580 sq. ft.)

Sample Text:

All buildings are located within the Corporate Center. The Center is located in an urban area of Anytown, USA. A mixture of light industry, professional office buildings, hotels, restaurants, and retail shops are in close proximity. The Corporate Center is near state highways Rt. 3 and Rt. 17 and the New Jersey Turnpike. The Sports Complex is located several miles east of the Corporate Center.

The buildings surveyed are between fifteen and twenty years old. The interior and exterior of the buildings are well maintained. The grounds and landscaping are also well maintained. A check of the properties and surrounding area found no visible sign of unauthorized congregation or quality-of-life crimes.

Executive Summary:

Persons Interviewed: John Doe
Building Manager
ABC Company

Jack Doe
Lead Technician
ABC Company

Mike Doe
Technician
ABC Company

Ralph Doe
Technician
ABC Company

Harry Doe
Technician
ABC Company

Mark Doe

Security Officer
ABC Security

Detective, Sergeant, etc.
Police Department

All Persons interviewed were helpful and courteous. All employees of ABC Company were knowledgeable and eager to assist with the survey. They represented ABC Company with a high degree of professionalism.

Additional information and data as needed.

Characteristics common to the following office buildings managed by ABC Company, and located in the Corporate Center

* * *

Hours of operation are 6:30 A.M. to 7:00 P.M.
All buildings are equipped with proximity key access controls located on the ground-floor common entrances.
All central monitoring and elevator phones are monitored.
All CCTV monitor systems include monitor, VCR, and multiplexer. All monitor systems are secured in a metal safe. The safes are secured by lock and key. Only security personnel have access to the safes.
All CCTV systems are color.
External cameras are not present.
A two-week videotape library is maintained.
CCTV systems operate 24/7.
CCTV systems are not monitored.
All cameras are in fixed locations.
Security personnel change videotapes daily.
All buildings are equipped with motion detectors at the ground-floor common entrances.
Access systems are installed on all ground-floor common entrances. Phone # 1-800-555-5555.
System was installed by XYZ Security 908-555-5555.

All systems have shunt overrides.

All system doors are equipped with magnetic locks.

All system doors have deadbolt key locks as backup.

Sara Doe and Jan Doe of ABC Company are responsible for the distribution of proximity access keys.

The computer and printer are located in Sara Doe's office.

All roof access doors are alarmed.

All master keys are marked "Do Not Duplicate."

Keys are available to building management personnel and cleaning personnel.

Sparkling Cleaning Co. cleans the buildings. They are located at 123 Any Street, Your Town, USA 12345 (555)-555-5555.

Professional Security provides security for the ABC Company buildings.

Professional Security is located at 123 Any Street, Your Town, USA 55555. Phone #555-555-5555.

Professional Security utilizes roving patrols in marked units. Walking patrols at several buildings support the roving patrols.

Patrol hours are as follows:

Monday – Friday
 2 Roving Patrols from 10 a.m. to 8 p.m.
 1 Walking Patrol from 3 p.m. to 7 p.m. at 1200 W.S.W.
 1 Walking Patrol from 2 p.m. to 6 p.m. at 1280 W.S.W.
 1 Walking Patrol from 2 p.m. to 6 p.m. at 210 Clay Ave

Saturday & Sunday
 1 Mobil Roving Patrol – 24 hour

Professional Security utilizes a touring system.

Security officers will escort upon request.

All common stairwell doors are unsecured.

There are no emergency phones in stairwells.

Emergency lighting is present in all stairwells and can be activated 24/7.

There are no exterior garbage areas.

All garbage and recyclables are transported by Sparkling Cleaning Co., to on-site compactors.

All women's restrooms are secured with combination pin-lock access controls.

All buildings are equipped with emergency generators that are tested periodically.

Security personnel are equipped with radios for communication.

None of the buildings have controls for visitors.

Sprinkler systems are installed throughout the buildings.

Fire extinguishers are available on every floor and inspections are up-to-date.

A general fire and life safety plan is in effect for each building.

Office Building Information

Street Address

The building has two common ground-floor entrances. The entrances consist of two sets of double glass doors separated by a small foyer. Two color CCTV cameras monitor the entrances.

Location – The electrical room is found here. Contained in the electrical room is the fire alarm and control panel. There are 21 active fire zones. Damage was observed on the door jam near the locking mechanism.

Location – Inspection of the ladies' restroom door and teledata room found them to be secure and free of damage.

Location – The men's and ladies' restrooms were secured with a pin combination lock. The doors were secure and no damage was observed.

Location – Damage to the doorjamb near the lock was observed on the teledata room door. The ladies' restroom was secure.

Location – The ladies' restroom and teledata room were secure and no signs of damage were observed.

The penthouse is accessed through a steel door. The door is alarmed with an audible alarm system. A vendor sign-in sheet is attached to the door. The alarm is set with a combination keypad. The penthouse contains the emergency generators. The Penthouse door was secure, and no damage was observed.

Exterior – There are three exterior access doors located in the building. These doors are all located on the ground floor. The first, a steel door, is located in the INS offices. The door has no exterior doorknob and can only be opened from inside. The other two doors provide access to an unoccupied former dance club. One of the doors is a single glass door with a deadbolt lock, and the other door is a steel service entrance door. All doors were secure.

There are two ground-floor common entrances. The entrances consist of two sets of double glass doors separated by a foyer. A color CCTV camera monitors each entrance.

Location – This floor contains the electrical room and teledata room. There is an elevator bank containing three elevators that stop at all five floors. The electric room contains an alarm and control box. There are 19 active fire zones. The teledata room contains the transmitter and the CCTV safe. A check found the ladies room secure.

Location – The ladies' restroom was found to be secure. Damage was found on the teledata room door and door jam.

Location – This floor contains a Cafeteria for DEF Company. A check of the teledata room found damage to the door and doorjamb. The ladies' restroom was secure.

Locations – Tenant-occupied by DEF Company. Access to the penthouse mechanical room is through tenant space. The penthouse door is alarmed with an audible alarm, which is also control-monitored. A logbook is attached to the door.

There are two ground-floor common entrances. The entrances consist of double glass doors separated by a foyer. A color CCTV camera monitors each entrance.

Location – The elevator room and maintenance room are located here. Pry mark damage was observed on the door of the elevator room. The maintenance room contains the fire alarm and control panel. The CCTV safe is also kept in this room.

Location – GHI Company occupies this floor. The office is alarmed, and a guard is on duty during the evening.

Location – The door to the women's restroom was secure. Pry damage was observed on the teledata room door.

Location – The door to the ladies' restroom was secure. Pry damage was observed on the teledata/electric room door.

Location – The control panels are located in the electric room.

Access to the roof is by a roof hatch. The hatch is not locked or secured. The hatch is alarmed and monitored.

There are two ground-floor common entrances. The entrances consist of double glass doors. A color CCTV camera monitors each entrance. There is an elevator bank, which consists of three elevators, including one service elevator. The first-floor maintenance room contains the fire alarm and control panel. There are twenty-two active fire zones. The CCTV safe is also located in this room.

Location – A small delicatessen (Deli in the Park) is located here. Pry mark damage was observed on the door jam of the teledata room. The women's restroom was secure.

Location – The women's restroom was secure. Damage was observed on the door and doorjamb of the teledata room.

Location – Unoccupied.

Location – The ladies' restroom was secure. There is damage to the door and doorjamb of the teledata/electric room.

Note: The west-side stairwell has tenant access on the second, third, and fourth floors. All tenant access doors are alarmed.

Location – The teledata and electric room doors show signs of pry tool damage. Access to the penthouse mechanical room is gained through a steel door that is equipped with an audible alarm. Access is gained by use of a numerical combination keypad. A central alarm is monitored. A contractor logbook is attached to the door.

Street Address

The building is divided into two wings that are referred to as the North Wing and the South Wing. A large atrium area separates these wings. DEF Company along with JKL Company predominantly occupy the building. There are six ground-floor common entrances. Access at each entrance is made through double glass doors. Four of these entrances allow direct entry into the common atrium. Each wing has one entrance into a common hallway.

A bank of four elevators is located in the Atrium. Each wing has a service elevator. A fire system control panel is located in the atrium area. There are 78 active zones. A service entrance is located at the South Wing. The access consists of double steel doors. The door is alarmed and monitored by a CCTV camera. Pry mark damage was observed on the main elevator room door.

A first-floor storage room in the North Wing contains the CCTV safe and the interface panel.

Street Address

This building is presently unoccupied. There is no access control system or CCTV located within the building. There is one common ground-floor entrance. There is a rear service door. There are three elevators, including a freight elevator. The rear service elevator is equipped with an audible alarm system, which is presently not operable. A CCTV camera had monitored the service elevator before it was disconnected. Access to the roof can be made through a roof hatch. This access does not have an alarm and is not secured.

Inventory Of CCTV Equipment In Office Buildings

Building Color Monitor Time Lapse VCR 9 Channel Multiplexer Street Address

Street Address

Street Address

Street Address

Street Address

Street Address

Street Address

Warehouse Building Information

Characteristics common to the following warehouse buildings, managed by ABC Company and located in the Corporate Center

All buildings are multi-tenant office and warehouse space.

There are no alarms or access controls on common entrances.

All primary common access doors are glass doors with deadbolt locks.

All buildings are equipped with fire alarm panels.

Central monitoring is conducted.

All buildings have exterior roof access, which consists of an exterior steel ladder contained within a locked ladder cage.

Warehouses are equipped with interior and exterior emergency lighting.

Tenants are responsible for their own security controls.

Professional Security supplies exterior security patrols.

All buildings are equipped with emergency sprinkler systems in case of fire.

There are no fences or physical barriers installed along the perimeter of the buildings.

All secondary access doors are metal.

All buildings are equipped with exterior lighting, which is attached to the building. Lighting is photocell-activated.

None of the warehouse buildings have exterior CCTV equipment.

Warehouse Tenants And Security Controls

Street Address

Tenant
Central monitoring system
10 interior skylights that are secured with steel bars
2 roof hatches, unsecured
No interior roof access
8 bay doors
3 secondary doors
All doors are alarmed

Tenant
Central monitor
3 bay doors
1 secondary access door

Tenant
5 bay doors
1 secondary access door

Tenant
Central monitor
2 bay doors
2 secondary access doors

Street Address

Tenant
Professional Security

Tenant
The Best Security

Tenant

Professional Security

Tenant
The Best Security

Tenant
Alarms

Street Address

Tenant
Professional Protection, central monitor
Bay doors and secondary access

Tenant
The Best Security, central monitor, audible
Bay doors and secondary access

Tenant
 Alarms, central monitor, motion detectors

Tenant
No security system

Street Address

Tenant
Central monitor
3 bay doors

Tenant
Professional Security, central monitor
5 bay doors
4 secondary doors

Tenant
The Best Security, central monitor

Street Address

Tenant
Professional Security System
No warehouse space

Tenant
The Best Security, central monitor

Tenant
Professional Security, central monitor

Tenant
The Best Security

Tenant
No security controls

Tenant
Professional Security, central monitor

Tenant
The Best central monitor
CCTV motion detectors
No warehouse space

Incident Reports

A review of incident reports generated by Professional Security and ABC Company personnel for the period of January 1, 1999 through September 10, 1999 shows the following incidents:

Thirteen (13) reported incidents of unsecured door found during non-business hours.

Five (5) reported incidents of small fires on or near the surveyed facilities.

Three (3) reported incidents of attempted vehicle theft.

Fire and Life Safety Guide

Mr. Doe advised me that the Safety Guide is being revised at this time. A review of the current Safety Guide found several omissions. The revised edition should include an emergency contact page. This page should include the contact numbers for the management team as well as the following numbers:

- Emergency ABC Security Company
- Fire Department Poison Control Center
- Ambulance Management Office
- Hospital Corporate Security

Security and Lighting

Parking Area and Lighting Survey for All Buildings

All parking areas are exterior, ground level, and paved lots. All parking areas were well maintained and free of debris. The lighting is photocell-activated. The following observations were made during an evening survey.

Street Address
There is poor illumination along the rear of the building on the south side.

Street Address
There is poor illumination at the front entrance (Wall St.). Illumination in the parking area is adequate.

Street Address
Adequate lighting.

Street Address

Spotlights over the entrance of (tenant name) were off, which caused poor illumination along one third of the building. The remainder of the parking area has adequate lighting.

Street Address
Adequate lighting.

Street Address
Southeast of building is dim. One spotlight found off. Remainder of area has adequate lighting.

Street Address
Adequate lighting.

Street Address
Adequate lighting.

Street Address
Adequate lighting in parking area. Rear southeast corner of building is dim. Adequate lighting in delivery area.

Street Address
Adequate lighting.

Street Address
Entrance light was out. Adequate lighting in parking area.

Law Enforcement

An interview was conducted (date, time, and location) with Detective Sergeant of the USA Town Police Department. Det. Sgt. advised me that the Corporate Center is a low-crime area. The Center is patrolled regularly with marked and unmarked police units. Det. Sgt. advised me that the most common crimes reported in the area were thefts and thefts from motor vehicles.

Police Statistics

From January 1, 1999 through September 20, 1999, the Police Department has responded to one hundred and eighty-five (185) alarm calls at the ABC Company buildings in the Corporate Center. Thefts were the most frequently reported crime (16), followed by theft from motor vehicles (5).

Requirements And Justification

Anytown, USA is a 4.7 square-mile municipality located in Any County, USA. The municipal characteristic is classified as Urban Suburb. The 1996 estimated population was 18,618. The police department consists of 46 sworn police officers.

The following crime index statistics were compiled and recorded in the 1998 Anytown USA Uniform Crime Report:

TOTAL VIOLENT/NON-VIOLENT CRIME RATE

Year	Crime Index	Per 1000	AGG.	M.V.
1997	551	18	533	29.6
1998	509	19	489	27.3

Year	Robbery	Assault	Burglary	Larceny	Theft
1997	6	10	90	332	111
1998	9	8	69	331	99

Cap Index ® registered Trademark of Cap Index, Inc. 20830 Valley Forge Circle, King of Prussia, PA 19406.

The CAP Index is a crime vulnerability assessment evaluation system designed to accurately identify the risk of personal and property crimes at any location in the United States. The Crimes Against

205

Persons and Crimes Against Property are the same crime types listed in the FBI's Uniform Crime Reports. The CAP Index is a weighted average of these crimes.

Site maps enhance the interpretation of the CAP Index assessment. The scoring methodology involves the use of two circles around the site in question: The first circle at a maximum of 1 (one) mile of a population of 25,000 people, and the second circle at a maximum radius of 3 (three) miles, or a population threshold of 100,000 people. Primary weight is given to the scores in the inner ring.

The Cap Index for this site is 72. There is no change from the 1990 Cap Index Score. The projected Cap Index for the years 2003-2004 is 73. The current state score for crimes against persons is 103. The state score for crimes against property is 152. The Cap Index and the site security survey indicate that these facilities should be at a Security Level II. Motor vehicle thefts appear to be the highest security risk. The current level of security is adequate, but the following recommendations should be considered.

RECOMMENDATIONS

Install security lock throw-cover plates on doors that afford access to the following:

Electric panels
Telephone/computer systems
Fire panels
Andover systems
CCTV
Elevator controls
Security systems

Update and distribute Fire & Life Safety Guide.
Repair damaged doors.
Install lighting in areas where needed.
Consider exterior CCTV in loading dock area of warehouses.
Notification should be sent to the tenants advising them of the following:

Advise tenants of excessive number of false alarms

Request tenants advise employees to be more attentive when securing doors and setting alarms

Request tenants remind employees to secure their personal items while in the building and lock their vehicles while parked on site 3

Attachments, photograph, floor plans, blueprints, etc.

SAMPLE SECURITY SURVEY – CHECKLIST FORMAT

This format was successfully utilized while conducting 153 Security Site Surveys nationwide for a recently merged professional practices firm, the largest such firm in the world. This format should be modified to meet the needs of the consult being conducted.

Elements of the Physical Security Review

Office Location:
Phone: Office Contact:
Phone: Real Estate Project. Mgr.:
Phone: Architect Project Mgr.:
Phone: Regional Director of Infrastructure (RDI):
Phone: Legacy co. [ ] Legacy co. [ ] Co-location [ ]
Remodel [ ] Other [ ] Describe:
Total square footage:
Number of employees at this site:
Lines of business at this location:
1. Hoteling? (visiting employees – short/long term?): yes [ ] no [ ]

Access System:

2. Electronic card access system: yes [ ] no [ ]
3. Y2K Compliance Certification letter attached: yes [ ] no [ ]
4. Date of access system installation
5. Mfg. name, type, model number,
6. Installation company name, address,
7. Installation company phone # and fax #
8. Installation company point of contact:
9. Access/CCTV system compatible with Base Building? yes [ ] no [ ]
10. Number of office card access readers:
11. Type of readers, i.e.: proximity, insert, swipe biometric, or numeric PIN

12. Number of doors protected, interior, perimeter:
13. Obtained activated sample of access card for reference? yes [ ] no [ ]
14. Are doors alarmed? yes [ ] no [ ]
15. Local sounding devices at doors? yes [ ] no [ ]
16. Door alarms to PC administering system only? yes [ ] no [ ]
17. Door alarms to central monitoring station? yes [ ] no [ ]
18. Attach copy of original installation proposal and contract yes [ ] no [ ]
19. Do doors automatically release and unlock during a fire alarm condition? yes [ ] no [ ]

Access System Administration – Monitoring

These questions must be asked of local company contact and security system vendors. The local office may not have the required information; contact the vendor in either case.

20. Electronic card access system administered by client or vendor?
21. Client [ ] Vendor [ ]
22. Approximate costs paid from date of installation by client for administration of system
23. Monthly cost for system administration
24. Monthly cost for system monitoring
25. Yearly system maintenance/service fees
26. What percentage of the original cost are the yearly maintenance fees?
27. Vendor contract reviewed for accuracy by reconciling office invoices against maintenance, monitoring and system administration fees. Provide detail in the body of your report. yes [ ] no [ ]
28. How are electronic access cards stored and administered? Ensure no "generic" cards are issued to vendors, clients, building security, building engineers, or cleaning staff. Does client policy mandate all cards be issued in the user's name

only and with access levels and hours appropriate for the individuals responsibilities?

29. If system is administered by client, how often is the system backed up and archived?

*In the event that there is no vendor service contract or the contract has lapsed or does not provide sufficient detail regarding costs broken down by category, request the vendor to provide the information in a timely manner.

CCTV System

30. CCTV; system in place client yes [ ] no [ ] Base Building yes [ ] no [ ] Installation company name, address, phone # and fax #

31. Installation company point of contact

32. Number of cameras

33. Black & White or Color? BW [ ] Color [ ]

34. Fixed or PZT? Fixed [ ] PZT [ ]

35. Describe in detail all components that comprise the CCTV system head-end; i.e., monitors, multiplexers, switchers, VCRs. Include manufacturer names, makes, and model #s of CCTV system. Who is responsible for changing tapes? How long are used tapes archived before being used again? When was the last time the videotapes were replaced with new ones?

36. When was the last time the VCRs were overhauled?

37. How many spare video inputs are available on the system head-end?

38. Original cost of CCTV system

39. Installation date of system

40. Year 2000-2005 compliant? yes [ ] no [ ]

41. Year 2000-2005 Compliance Certification letter attached yes [ ] no [ ]

42. Vendor will forward manufacturer's compliance letter/statement yes [ ] no [ ]

43. Yearly CCTV maintenance costs

44. List separate CCTV repair costs if they are not included in the maintenance costs.

Burglar Alarm System

45. Electronic burglar alarm system? yes [ ] no [ ]
46. Year 2000-2005 Compliance Certification letter attached yes [ ] no [ ]
47. Vendor will forward the manufacturer's compliance letter/statement yes [ ] no [ ]
48. Date of burglar alarm system installation
49. Mfg. name, type and model #
50. Installation company's name, address, phone # and fax #
51. Installation company point of contact
52. Installation cost of original burglar system
53. Is system compatible with Base Building system? yes [ ] no [ ]
54. Number and description of zones
55. Is the burglar alarm system integrated with the access control system? yes [ ] no [ ]
56. Are alarms connected to a central monitoring station? If not, include in body of report? yes [ ] no [ ]
57. Alarm monitoring company's name, address, phone and fax #
58. Monitoring company point of contact
59. Attach copy of original installation proposal and central station monitoring contract? yes [ ] no [ ]

Fire Alarm System

60. Electronic fire alarm system? yes [ ] no [ ]
61. Stand-alone system (or part of Base Bldg. System)? yes [ ] no [ ]
62. Year 2000-2005 Compliance Certification letter attached yes [ ] no [ ]
63. Vendor will forward the manufacturer's compliance letter/statement? yes [ ] no [ ]
64. Date of fire alarm system installation
65. Manufacturer's name, type and model # from control panel

66. Installation company name, address, phone # and fax #
67. Installation company point of contact
68. Connected to Base Building? yes [ ] no [ ]
69. Number and description of zones
70. Is the fire alarm system integrated with the access control system? yes [ ] no [ ]
71. Alarms connected to a central monitoring station? yes [ ] no [ ]
72. Alarms monitored by Base Bldg? yes [ ] no [ ]
73. Monitoring company name, address, phone # and fax #
74. Monitoring company point of contact
75. Attach copy of original installation proposal contract yes [ ] no [ ]
76. Distance to nearest fire department

Office Lease – Attach current and accurate client floor plans

77. Year and month of lease expiration

The following questions should be asked of the Real Estate Project Manager:
Future expansion of space planned or other construction projects? yes [ ] no [ ]
Future reduction of space planned? yes [ ] no [ ]
Include details of above plans in body of report

Base Building

78. Building Management
79. Contact Person/Title
80. Phone #/Fax #
81. Include building description and surrounding neighbor-hood description in the body of your report; i.e., Class A building in central downtown business district, floors 7 through 8.
82. Salient features of building: i.e., daycare, restaurants, shopping malls, etc.:
83. Current and projected use of building

84. If a warehouse, is lighting and fencing adequate and unobstructed? yes [ ] no [ ]
85. Is there adequate lighting for night operations? yes [ ] no [ ]
86. Does lease include security language/provisions? yes [ ] no [ ]
87. Comment on lease security language in the body of your report
88. Contract or proprietary security guards present? yes [ ] no[ ] Contract? [ ] Proprietary? [ ]
89. Do guards routinely patrol client space? If yes, please attach post orders yes [ ] no [ ] Number of guards and schedules:
90. Guard company name, address, phone # and fax #
91. Guard company contact person:
92. Base Building security includes:
93. CCTV – list locations in body of report yes [ ] no [ ] recorded [ ] reviewed [ ]
94. Electronic card access system? yes [ ] no [ ]
95. Fire alarm? yes [ ] no [ ]
96. Burglar alarm (list locations in body of report)? yes [ ] no [ ]
97. Other – if yes please describe in body of report; yes [ ] no [ ]
98. Which systems are compatible with client systems? Detail in body of report
99. Describe parking lot security and lighting systems
100. Is an escort available? yes [ ] no [ ]

* If guard services are billed back to the tenant, or if this office retains its own security guard company, review a sampling of monthly bills for accuracy, review guard placement, post-orders and supervision for efficiency and effectiveness in providing client reasonable coverage. Comment on the findings in the body of your report.

Local Law Enforcement

101. Name of agency and address
102. Contact name and phone #
103. Person interviewed and title
104. Distance to police department

Theft and Major Incident History

105. Local office contact name and phone #

* When interviewing the local office contact, capture the office history of computer theft, incidental theft, and related incidents. Review employee parking areas, after hours coming and going, street and parking lot lighting, neighborhood vagrants, drug dealing, etc. Include any security issues that might affect the safety or security of employees or threatens the security of the office in any manner.

Additional information, data and attachments as needed.

SAMPLE SECURITY SURVEY – <mark>TYPE 3</mark> – <mark>FILL-IN</mark>

CONFIDENTIAL - When Filled In

Your Security Company Name

Primary Site Security Checklist

1.0 Setup Information Client's Building Number:

Building Name:
Street Address:
City, State, Zip:
Client's Floors Occupied:
Client's Total Square Footage:
Building Owner:
Building Manager:
Building Representative(s);
Representative(s) Telephone, Fax, Pager Numbers:
Representative(s) Physical Location:
Building Point of Contact:
Client's Telephone, Fax, Pager Numbers:
Facility Functions:
Stories above ground:
Stories below ground:
Date of Construction:
Approximate Age:
Additional data:

Four Cross Streets that bound building:

North

South

East

West

Surrounding area description:
Distance in miles to nearest police station:
Distance in miles to nearest fire station:
Other occupying organizations - size and type:

Current use of office:

Projected use of office:

1.5 Number of non-Client's employees; e.g., contractors, out-sources, visitors, etc.
1.5.1 Number of visitors to Client's site on a daily basis:
1.5.2 Location(s) of visitor control point:
Salient features of Building; e.g., day-care center, commercial enterprises utilizing building.
1.6 – intentionally left blank.
1.7 Current or projected use of building; e.g., warehouse, office, etc.
1.7.1 If a warehouse, is loading dock area surrounded by wire fence?
1.7.2 If yes, is fence in good shape, not more than 2 inches from corner post or end post to end post?
1.7.3 Is all underbrush cleared away to provide unobstructed view of fence line?
1.7.4 Is there sufficient outdoor lighting for night operations?
1.7.5 Are fence gates, mechanical or electrical, in good order?
1.7.6 Are the fence outriggers in good shape and completely wired?
1.7.7 Is employee parking incorporated within the fenced-in area?
1.7.8 How does employee access the gate?
1.7.9 Do employees egress through the gate?
1.8 What is the general physical shape of the building's exterior?
1.8.1 Are examined doors in working order?
1.8.2 Are all locks on the exterior doors in good working order?
1.8.3 Are the locks on the examined doors compliant with OSHA regulations for fire exits?
1.8.4 What is the base fire suppression system?

1.8.5 Is the fire alarm system in good working order?

1.8.6 Where is the master control panel located?

1.8.7 Is it manned? If so, when?

1.8.8 Does the fire panel open all locked doors while alarm is activated?

1.8.9 Is the system fail-safe or fail secure or a combination thereof? Is there a written security plan or disaster preparedness plan? Last revision date?

2.00 Access Control

2.1 What are the normal building working/access hours? Are security guards present to control access? Who controls the security guards?

2.2 Do the uniformed security have a written operating procedure when to and how to respond to a Client's alarm or request for assistance?

2.2.1 Is the standard procedure manual reviewed and revised every two years by management?

2.2.2 Are guards contract or privately owned by building management or Client?

2.2.3 How many in each shift?

2.2.4 Are guards present while Client's employees are working?

2.2.5 Do shifts cover 24/7?

2.2.6 Where are employee and visitor parking in relation to this building?

2.2.7 How is access to the parking area controlled?

2.2.8 Identify all entry and exit points from stairwells:

2.2.9 Are these doors alarmed? If so, how?

2.3 Identify all emergency exit points from ground floor offices:

2.3.1 Identify all emergency exit points from below ground floor:

2.3.2 Are these doors alarmed? If so, how?

2.3.3 Identify primary entry/exit control points for all employees:

2.3.4 Are these doors alarmed? If so, how?

2.3.5 Identify primary entry/exit control points for all visitors: 2.36 Are these doors alarmed? If so, how?

2.3.6 Is badging required for building access? If so, what type?

2.3.7 Who owns/controls the badging system?

2.3.8 Are the badges kept in a secure place?

2.3.9 Who has oversight of the badging system?

2.4 Can Client's employees access their work areas with a single badge? If not, why not?

2.4.1 Are Client's badging schemes similar to badging in Client's other offices?

2.4.2 Do badges reflect the building/company name and address?

2.4.3 Are stairwells regularly used by the Client's employees for between-floor access? If so, are the entry doors on an access device?

2.4.4 Once in the stairwell, is the only way out, without an access pass, at the ground floor level?

2.4.5 Are the stairwells used by employees on the lower levels to exit at quitting times?

2.4.6 Identify all passenger and freight elevators and which Client's floors they have access to:

2.4.7 Identify which elevators are locked out after hours and who controls the keys:

2.4.8 Do janitors have access to all or some of the elevators after hours?

2.4.9 Who controls and distributes the janitors' keys?

2.5 How are the janitors identified?

2.5.1 Are there basic background investigations completed on the janitors who work in the Client's areas by the janitorial company?

2.5.2 Are the janitors under constant supervision by their employers while in Client's areas?

2.5.3 Are janitors given permanent keys, ID cards? If so, who issues and controls them?

2.5.4 Are any "no-name" ID cards issued to people other than visitors?

2.5.5 Locate all shipping and receiving docks:

2.5.6 Who controls them?

2.5.7 When do they operate?

2.5.8 What do they do for delivery after hours?

2.5.9 What is the small-parcel program?

2.6.0 Identify all cafeteria and lunchrooms:

2.6.1 Do they have vending machines?

2.6.2 Identify all vending machine areas on each floor:

2.6.3 How are supplies brought in?

2.6.4 Are permanent passes or ID cards/keys issued to vendors?

2.6.5 Are they escorted while in Client's areas? If so, by whom?

2.6.6 How is mail brought into the building?

2.6.7 Is there a single point of mail distribution for the Client? 2.83 Who distributes the Client's mail?

2.6.8 What are the mailroom hours of service?

2.6.9 Identify central file room(s):

2.7.0 Are the doors and service windows alarmed?

2.71 Identify HR file room:

2.7.2 Are the doors and service windows alarmed?

2.7.3 Identify airline ticket printing machine room:

2.74 Are the doors and service windows alarmed?

2.7.5 Where are the service trucks required to park?

2.7.6 Are the persons performing a service in Client's areas badged and/or under constant escort?

2.7.7 Where is the trash/garbage placed?

2.7.8 Is it secured from "Dumpster Diving"?

2.7.9 How do trash pickup personnel and vehicles get to it?

2.8.0 Locate all ground-level air-handling facilities, particularly air intake vents:

2.8.1 Identify mechanical rooms; are they locked? If so, who controls the keys?

2.8.2 Identify tele/data rooms; are they locked? If so, who controls the keys?

2.8.3 Identify security panel rooms; are they locked? If so, who controls the keys?

2.8.4 How do service personnel obtain access to these areas?

2.8.5 Identify PBX services room; is it locked? If so, who controls the keys?

2.8.6 Identify the DEMARK room:

2.8.7 Who has access to this room and how is it controlled?

3.00 Key Control

3.1 Who has control of the master and sub-master level keys? Who is responsible for key control?

3.1.1 Who is responsible for changing locks, combinations?

3.1.2 Are keys and combinations not authorized for duplication?

3.1.3 Do any safes containing cash, bonds, or other high-value items have a UL rating? If so, are certificates available?

3.1.4 Is there a "cashiers" station?

3.15 If so, is this station provided due security based on SEC or other security guidelines being utilized?

3.16 Does this station satisfy those requirements?

3.2 Are keypad (pin)/cipher locks used anywhere in Client's areas? How often are the ciphers changed, and by whom?

3.2.1 Where are the cipher keys kept?

3.3 Card Access Readers

3.3.1 Are card access readers used anywhere in Client's areas in the building?

3.3.2 Where are the card access readers terminated?

3.3.3 Who is the manufacturer of the card access readers?

3.3.4 Is the card access system Y2K certified?

3.3.5 Who installed the readers and when?

3.3.6 Who owns the readers?

3.3.7 Will they allow a Client's employee to utilize the same reading device to enter other Client's buildings? Are they capable of such?

3.3.8 Are the card entry devices and the ID card one in the same or two separate items?

3.3.9 Does a Client's employee need more than one entry device to enter Client's areas? If so, why?

3.4 Does each Client floor have a reception area?

3.4.1 Does each Client reception area have a "buzz-in" capability?

3.4.2 Does each Client reception area have a "panic" button to call for assistance?

4.0 Alarms

4.1 Are any ground-level doors alarmed with a local fire alarm if door is opened?

4.1.1 Are any ground-level doors alarmed which report to a monitored panel?

4.1.2 Are any interior doors alarmed which report to a monitored panel?

4.1.3 If alarms are monitored, where are they monitored and when is it manned?

4.1.4 If alarms are monitored by a contract security company, what is the expiration date of the contract?

4.1.5 Is the above contract part of a lease agreement?

4.1.6 Does the uniformed guard service respond to any Client's alarms? If not, why not, and who does?

4.1.7 Are there any duress "panic" alarms not mentioned above?

4.1.8 Where are the duress alarms monitored?

4.1.9 Are any alarms monitored directly by a law enforcement agency?

4.2 How long does it take a law enforcement agency to respond to an alarm?

4.2.1 Are there documented tests being conducted at least annually?

4.2.2 If there is a central station monitoring, where is the location and who maintains it?

4.2.2.1 Is the central station monitoring part of the lease?

4.2.3 Are there dual motion sensors placed in critical areas?

4.2.4 Are there dual glass break sensors placed in areas where glass breakage would allow fast entry to a Client's work area?

4.2.5 Are Client's employees protected from flying glass shards, should a window break accidentally?

4.2.5.1 Does the computer server room have glass windows which, when broken, could cause severe damage to a computer?

4.2.5.2 Could glass breakage in the computer server room give someone quick access to the server?

4.2.5.3 Does the computer server room have the necessary water, heat, smoke, fire, and motion detectors installed?

4.3 Have all critical areas been identified and are they properly alarmed?

5.0 CCTV

5.1 Is there CCTV in the base building areas?

5.1.1 Is there CCTV in the Client's occupied areas?

5.2 Where is the CCTV monitored?

5.2.1 If monitored at the guard desk or at the reception desk, do monitors face away from visitors and employees?

5.2.2 Are CCTV signal feeds sent to a remote monitoring station?

5.2.2.1 If so, which camera feeds are sent?

5.2.2.2 Are they sent on a 24/7 hours basis or only during normal working hours?

5.2.2.3 Are any CCTV signals switch to alarmed mode doors? Are the CCTV signals taped?

5.2.4 Are tapes being kept for 30 days, grandfathered and used again?

5.2.4.1 Are tapes kept in a secure lock-and-key storage location? Who secures and keeps track of the tapes?

5.2.4.2 Are signs in a conspicuous location indicating CCTV is in use?

5.2.5 Who owns the CCTV system (including VCR, MUX and monitor)? If leased, when does the current lease expire?

Does building management share in costs?

Are there any perimeter cameras?

Are they fixed or pan-tilt-zoom?

Who owns those cameras?

Are they leased? If so when does lease expire?

Is there CCTV in the garage area?

Is there CCTV on the roof area?

Is there CCTV at the stairwells?

5.2.6 Is there CCTV in the interior watching the fire doors? Is there CCTV in the lobby area?

Is there any in the day-care center?

Is there CCTV on the loading dock(s)?

Is there CCTV located near card readers?

Is there CCTV located in critical areas?

Is there CCTV located in all reception areas?

Has the system, VCR, been maintained annually?

Is the CCTV black and white or color?
Does building management share it?
Is the CCTV system Y2K certified?
Is certification attached?

6.0 Client Security Systems Administration

6.1 What was the original cost of the security system?

6.1.1 Is the system Y2K compliant? If yes, is there certification?

6.1.2 What is the monthly cost for system administration?

6.1.3 What are the monthly costs for system monitoring?

6.1.4 What are the yearly system maintenance fees of original capital costs?

6.2 When was the system installed and turned over as operational?

6.2.1 Is the MUX system capable of expansion? If so, how many ports?

6.2.2 What is the make and model of the MUX system? Are the cameras digital or analog?

6.2.3 Is cabling secured in conduit when in "open" areas? Are camera mounts accessible without a ladder?

6.2.4 Can the cameras be easily pulled down from brackets? Are all cameras placed within housings?

7.0 Security Assessment

7.1 Is CAP Index, Inc.® data sheet attached?

7.1.1 Is CAP Index, Inc. map sheet attached?

7.0 Based on this facility's Client mission, e.g. government contracts, etc., and the CAP Index ratings, does this facility meet?

7.2.1 LEVEL I – Low: Only physical key or cipher key entry required. CAP Index level U-50

7.2.2 LEVEL II – CAP Index Level 50-99: Electronic burglar alarm system, perimeter doors and windows protected, motion detectors, panic buttons at reception desk, if teledata rooms are present, water, temp alarms, PC storage/repair or client and/or server information computers are housed in this facility.

7.2.3 LEVEL III – CAP Index Level 100-199: In addition to Level I and II requirements, electronic access control with door-held-open alarms on perimeter doors and/or high risk/critical interior doors.

7.2.4   LEVEL IV – CAP Index 200-499: In addition to Level I– III requirements, CCTV is added to "exit/entrance only" basis, based on a risk factor as a result of this completed survey and in consultation with local and national representatives.

7.2.5 LEVEL V – CAP Index 500+: In addition to Level I– IV requirements, this level is only reached after consultation with all parties concerned as to the risk, vulnerability and consequence factors. The highest level of security is to be implemented in any of Client's locations.

7.2.6 In addition to any level of security, it may be necessary to implement and incorporate a video badging system (VBS) into the base security plan at any level, provided based on a number of variables. This VBS may be a stand-alone or may be "networked" with a number of Client's facilities, which would allow the user to enter any Client's building and access equivalent areas, as he/she would have at the "home" site. The VBS would incorporate a standardized badge for each employee, contractor, resident client, partner, and visitor and whether or not they are authorized a temporary access or require an escort.

8.0 Accommodations

8.1 Client's preferred hotel:

8.1.1 Hotel's direct reservation telephone number:

8.1.2 Is direct billing available to the client for the hotel?

8.1.3 How far is hotel from Client's building?

8.1.4 Is airport limousine service available?

8.1.5 Is Client provided "shuttle" service from hotel? From/to other locations (please state)?

8.1.6 Is a rental car recommended or appropriate for this location?

SAMPLE SECURITY SURVEY – TYPE IV

The following survey/audit uses a numerical averaging system to provide the security consultant and client with an objective "self-proving" document. Directions on how to complete the audit form appear in the legend at the end of the survey.

Security Survey – Audit/Numerical Evaluation

Your Security Company, Inc.
Security Audit Checklist
Facility: Name + Address
Date: Of Survey Item Number: Unique ID#
Description + Location:
Operational Score Consequence Score
1-A Identification of Critical Areas (Items)
1.0 Computer Equipment
  1.1 Computer Storage Room
  1.2 Computer Burn-in Room
  1.3 Computer Repair Room
  1.4 Computer Server Room
  1.5 Tel/Data Closets
  1.6 Security Closets
  1.7 CCTV Control Room
  1.8 Mail Room
  1.9 PBX Room
  2.0 Restricted Rooms
  2.1 Director Central Intelligence Approved Rooms
  2.2 Central File Room
  2.3 HR File Records Room
  2.4 ID Camera Storage Room
  2.5 ID Badge Supply Storage Room
  1-B Analysis of Threat
  1.00 CAP Index, Inc.
  2.0 Natural Disaster History
  3.0 Law Enforcement Information
  3.1 Local Law Enforcement Response

3.2 Local Law Enforcement Location
3.3 In-House Loss Prevention
3.3.1 In-House Loss Identified
3.3.2 In-House Loss Recovered
3.3.3 Facility Security Manual – Current (2 yrs)
1-C Analysis of Vulnerabilities
1.00 Adversarial View of Location, Soft vs. Hard
2.0 Guard Services
2.1 Contract Services
2.2 In-House Services
2.2.1 Appearance
2.2.2 Attitude
2.2.3 Response Capabilities
2.2.4 Armed / Not Armed
2.2.5 State Certified
2.2.6 Criminal Background Conducted
2.2.7 Training Verified
2.2.8 Client Uniformed Guard – Instructions (Current)
2.2.9 LEA – Current or Former Officer
2.3 Communications – Radio
2.3.1 Communications – Telephone
2.3.2 Communications – Cell Phone
2.3.3 Personal Panic/Help Device
2.3.4 Guard Post(s)
2.3.5 Logical Locations
2.3.6 Co-Located Service with Building Management Svc
2.3.7 Guard Back-up Availability
2.3.8 Guard Supervision on-site
2.3.9 Guard Duty Availability (24/7)
2.4 Off-Duty Location
2.4.1 Guard Intervention History
2.4.2 Costing to Client
2.4.3 Costing Shared
3.0 Fire Prevention and Suppression
3.1 Nearest Fire Station
3.2 Fire Station Response Time
3.3 Base Building / Client Fire Calls

4.0 Base Building Fire Suppression System

4.1 Meets Y2K

4.2 Meets State/Local fire codes

4.3 Systems tests documented

4.4 Doors fail-safe / fail-secure

4.5 Fire Systems Tied into Central Monitor or Fire Sta.

5.0 Locking Device Control

5.1 Physical Key Control

5.2 Lock and Key Storage Container

5.3 Physical Keys Labeled as to Location

5.4 Keys Signed Out and Receipted For

5.5 Keys Inventoried at Shift Change

5.6 Keys under client control

6.0 Electronic Keypad System

6.1 Integrated with ID Card System

6.2 Tracked by Employee Number

6.3 System Owned/Leased

6.4 System Install Date

6.5 System Costing

6.6 System Controlled in-house

6.7 System Controlled at vendor site

7.0 Electronic Key System Locations

7.1 Main Entrance(s)

7.2 Side Entrance(s)

7.3 Rear Entrance(s)

7.4 Loading Dock (s)

7.5 Fire Door Exit (s)

7.6 Floor Entrance(s)

8.0 Other Critical Sites – not previously identified

8.1 Travel – Ticket Writing Machine

8.2 Cashier's Station

8.3 Client's File Vault

8.4 HR Records Room

9.0 Other

10.0 Exterior Fence

10.1 Fence in good working order

10.2 Fence gate in good operation

10.3 No more than two inches between stand posts
10.4 Outriggers up and wired
10.5 Overgrowth cleared on both sides of fence
11.0 Exterior Lighting
11.1 Exterior lighting – overlapping cones of light
11.2 Lights shine away from windows
11.3 Lights provide sufficient light in parking area/garage
11.4 All lights in good working order
12.0 Exterior Doors / Glazing
12.1 Exterior glazing is/is not cracked or broken
12.2 Exterior glazing has burglar resistant film, Plexiglas, or other protection from quick entry/exit
12.3 Exterior doors open/close and lock correctly
12.4 Exterior doors have audible alarms IAW local fire

Risk = Threat + Vulnerability + Consequence

Ops Score = Operational Condition Index #DIV/0!
   0 = Not observed or Not Applicable
   1 = Excellent Working Order or Condition
   2 = Good Working Order or Condition
   3 = Missing, needs replacement, or poor working condition

Consequence Score Index

   0 = No consequence if not working or available
   1 = Minimal consequence to Client's operations if not working/available
   2 = Some consequence to Client's operations if not working/available
   3 = Major consequence to Client's operations if not working/available

Consequence is determined to be anything that effects Client's daily operations, from minimal inconveniences to major disruptions.

Note: The "Index" is an average of the Vulnerability scores and Consequence scores. Protection required is based on safety of personnel, loss of equipment through loss or theft, loss/theft of Client's proprietary data, and other potential disruptions to business.

Based on the above formula, the RISK Factor for this facility is shown herein (from crime report figures, FBI/UCR): Threat Index, Vulnerability Index, Consequence Index. The higher the risk factor, the greater the risk to conduct client business.

Risk Factor:

LEVEL I 50
LEVEL II 50–90
LEVEL III 100–199
LEVEL IV 200–499
LEVEL V 500 +

Note: The Vulnerability Factor and Consequence Factor are based on the averages of those scores as assigned by the security consultant; thus, a realistic risk index is achieved

Chapter Fourteen

Total Quality Consulting

As we face trying times and unprecedented threat to our national freedoms, it seems the ideal time to address how we, as leaders, are going to lead, direct, manage, supervise, and motivate for success.

The decades of the 1980s and 1990s clearly demonstrated that clients and customers demand and expect service. Now is the time to evaluate ourselves, our organizations, and those around us. As we conduct this evaluation, we are going to discover discrepancies and shortcomings. This "discovery" is a positive first step in improving quality. Improved quality, in turn, improves all aspects of the work environment, from basic working conditions to the bottom-line and everything in between. The successful leaders are going to be those individuals that keep current on changing technologies, maintain their professional development, and share that knowledge with others.

In this section, I attempt to remind leaders and potential leaders of things they already know, or should already know. There are no charts, diagrams, or lessons. Rather, a common-sense, KISS (keep it simple, stupid) principle approach to leadership. Reminders of how people, customers, and employees alike, want to be treated. To lead you, must first follow. The successful leader will be a skilled follower, trustworthy, honorable, loyal, and dedicated. He is going to be fair, firm, and honest. He will have the courage to make the tough calls and the courage of his convictions. His integrity will never be in doubt, professionally or personally. He will lead by positive example.

I have had the good fortune of attending several top-notch leadership development programs and to serve as an instructor of TQM for the U.S. Air Force and of leadership development at Valley Forge Military College, a school with a well-deserved global reputation for character and leadership development. I have also had the great honor and distinct privilege to command troops worldwide in frequently remote locations while facing hazardous conditions. During my tenure as an Air Force unit commander, we won several prestigious awards for outstanding performance. This success was due exclusively to the tremendous efforts of the whole team. This success, like all successes, depends on the efforts of the team. It is your function as the leader to take care of the team and they, in turn, will take care of you.

My attempt is to present you a reminder to do the right thing, say the right thing—and mean it—and to support others in their attempts to do the right thing. You will see several quotes and examples within this section that I hope will give you pause to ask, "Is what I'm about to do or say the right thing, the honorable thing? Is this how I would like to be treated?"

Quality Service

Successful organizations recognize the need to improve and wisely adapt to changing demands. Service firms are no exception. Facing a dynamic international environment with shrinking resources, today's company will undergo fundamental changes.

The quality approach provides a framework to assist your organization in improving while you adjust. You must find the means to improve the way you conduct business. That is where quality will help, allowing you to improve productivity through the collective skills, strength, determination, and ingenuity of all. Teamwork! As an added bonus, you will assist your client in two ways: providing your service and introducing them to quality through your example. The U.S. General Accounting Office (GAO) conducted an analysis of companies embracing quality-management principles and found, "performance indicators in each area GAO studied showed an overall average annual improvement from the time companies adopted Total Quality Management (TQM) to the publication of the latest available data." Quality works!

What Is Quality Leadership?

Leadership is the art of supervising, managing, directing, and influencing people in a manner that inspires confidence and wins respect, loyalty, and obedience in achieving a common objective.

Strong quality leadership is a key attribute of TQM. Many of the principles and practices that are required in a quality environment might be contrary to entrenched practice. Only a strong leadership team with the determination and courage to drive and accept change will be successful. A philosophy of continuous improvement is the fundamental attribute that drives quality. Action based on facts, data, and analysis and a willingness to measure quality are the tools utilized to adapt to the changes required to continue seeking greater quality.

First and foremost, quality is a commitment, and that commitment becomes your operating style. Your commitment and style will inspire continuous improvement, trust, and teamwork everywhere in the organization. It's a way of controlling the style and shape of your future. It's the wisdom to know that different situations call for different leadership styles and the skill to know when and how to apply those styles. Dr. Thomas E. Cronin, a distinguished college president and professor of American institutions and leadership at Colorado College, focuses on many of the different facets of leadership and suggests, "Different kinds of leaders may be appropriate for different kinds of situations." Successful leaders are those who can adapt their behavior to meet the demands of their particular situation. There are always opportunities to improve functions and operations. Those around you, at all levels, will appreciate attempts to improve the system. Quality techniques and principles provide you with the needed tools for making those improvements. These concepts have a proven track record in world-class organizations around the globe. Put simply, it works!

Leadership is the foundation of the quality system. Without leadership, the foundation will crumble. Why? Leaders establish the policies, priorities, the vision, tactics, and strategies. Leaders create an environment that inspires pride, trust, and teamwork. Leaders create and maintain a system perspective and a customer focus. Leaders don't lose sight of their overall responsibilities. Leaders don't lose their composure. They have command presence, a certain "grace under fire." They have the ability to absorb the heat from above without passing it to those below. These responsibilities can't be delegated.

Situational Leadership

The situation will frequently dictate the type of leadership appropriate to the task at hand. Successful leaders are those who can adapt their behavior to meet the requirements of their particular situation. Over the past few decades, people in leadership positions have looked for the "best" style of leadership. Numerous studies have reflected that there is no single all-purpose leadership style. Drs. Ken Blanchard and Paul Hersey developed the Situational Leadership Theory. This theory is based on the amount of direction (task behavior) and the amount of supportive (relationship) behavior a leader must provide in a given situation and the level of maturity (readiness) of the follower or group. To determine the level of maturity, you must first know the follower's level of ability and willingness. As an example, in a learning environment, perhaps the democratic leadership style is best, as this is a time when the interface between student and teacher will foster success. However, on the battlefield or in the midst of fighting a raging fire, we can assume that the autocratic style would be most effective. In the research laboratory, the freedoms of the laissez-faire style will provide the forum for the free expression of the creative scientist. The same can be said for personal or professional development. Leadership styles can and will change as people develop or regress. A more hands-on approach is going to be more appropriate for the entry-level beginner, and less personal attention will be required for the highly experienced worker. So the situation can, and frequently does, decide the best leadership approach.

Quality System

The quality system is an integrated system of three components built on leadership. Leadership and management are not the same. Drive past any shopping mall and you will see scores of signs posted by companies advertising "managers wanted and management positions available." Being vested with the title Manager does not automatically establish one as a leader. Position or rank does not automatically establish leadership. Leaders lead and managers manage. People follow leaders; they may or may not elect to obey managers. Some have said "leaders lead people, managers manage functions." This is not to imply that the important tasks of managers, accounting and inventory control, for example, are less important—clearly they are not. Quality can and should be applied to functional management demands also.

Leaders are found at all levels, including the entry-level "new guy." Leaders are those who have made a personal commitment to improve themselves, their workplace, their home, their surroundings, wherever they might be. They are people with a healthy dissatisfaction for the way things are. They know that "if you always do what you've always done, you'll always get what you've always gotten." They have the courage to fail, as well as a desire and plan for success. Take as an example, the manager of a fast food restaurant. It's noon and the store is crowded to overflowing. The manager, demonstrating leadership, steps in to assist his staff, he maintains his composure, he asks rather than demands, he supports and works alongside his employees, and the staff reacts favorably by following his lead. Functioning as a team, they all give a little extra effort, and after the rush they jointly celebrate their success—that's teamwork!

Be a leader, not a manager. Reginald Jones, former CEO at General Electric, said, "The world of the 1990s and beyond will not belong to 'managers' or those who can make the numbers dance. The world will belong to passionate, driven leaders—people who not only have enormous amounts of energy but can energize those whom they lead."

System Elements

Quality focus, the improvement process, and quality in routine operations are the system elements. Quality focus identifies the priority issues, while the improvement process directs continuous improvement efforts on the priorities you have identified. Finally, quality in routine activities applies quality concepts to the workplace.

Quality Focus

Strategic planning, senior-level guidance, and a cultural implementation throughout the organization—that's quality focus. This is an overall approach to quality, a complete alignment of goals and objectives. Planning should involve leaders at all levels as well as the frontline personnel. This way, there' s acceptance and commitment by all. When the ideas of people who know the process best are incorporated into planning, they are anxious to join the team. This is one of the cornerstones of team building. When planning, consider the following: does everyone know the plans and strategies, do they understand how they relate to the vision and mission, and do they know how their individual jobs relate to the overall operation? The answers to these questions are critical to the success of your organization.

Improvement Process

Teamwork and a disciplined approach of facilitating people working together toward a common goal—that is the improvement process. The improvement process is a workplace enriched by empowerment and individual participation supported by the true spirit of teamwork. The improvement process fosters greater individual and team skills, increases productivity, provides better services and products, opens communications, and creates a more pleasant atmosphere for all, company and clients alike. There is always room for improvement. Remember, maintain a healthy dissatisfaction for the way things are, a positive attitude, a sense of humor, and respect for those around you—at all levels.

Quality Operations

Your goal in the daily routine is to put the theoretical into operational practice. Here is where everyone takes their ideas and what they've learned and puts it to work. In a way, this is a test. Measurements and tools are needed here. The team, working together, makes improvement part of the job. Ed Koch, former mayor of New York City, said it best when he continuously asked, "How am I doin'?' He was measuring by requesting feedback, always seeking to improve, trying to satisfy his customers, the citizens and visitors of New York. Feedback is a critical element of communication.

Instill these elements in your organization and, with a lot of hard work, imagination, and creativity, you're guaranteed a better organization.

Summary

As we prepare to face the challenges ahead, we as leaders need to prepare for change, reflect on our vision and mission, and approach the future with determination, strength, zeal, and integrity. The successful organization of the future will be the organization that consistently meets or exceeds the requirements and expectations of their customers. The successful leader will be that highly principled individual who possesses the courage and wisdom to lead with exemplary behavior and the skill to assemble a world-class team of highly motivated and dedicated members.

The Quality Service Organization

My background was primarily in the public sector—military and law enforcement. It was while I was still with the government that I developed a true appreciation for attention to detail, professional development, customer satisfaction, and total quality management.

I learned that we all have customers, both internal and external. Someone is in need of what we have to offer, regardless of our rank, position, or function within the organization. I have had the great pleasure and privilege to serve with true leaders, men and women of character, selfless people, people dedicated to something bigger than themselves. I learned a great deal from these mentors. Tom Gallagher, retired director of the Pennsylvania State Bureau of Criminal Investigation, taught me firsthand that courage, honor, pride, and command presence are essential attributes of the great leader. Bob Harris, Major General, U.S. Air Force, the former Commander of the Pennsylvania Air National Guard, and the Deputy Adjutant General of Pennsylvania, set a sterling example of just how important respect, morality, quality, and personal demeanor are when dealing with others. I learned that all great leaders shared several characteristics, among them, dignity, honor, pride, integrity, courage, morality, and ethics.

As odd as this may seem, I also learned a great deal from people for whom I have absolutely no respect. I call these people the ethically challenged. I once had the displeasure of working for an "ethically challenged" supervisor who was a coward. I often marveled at how a person like this could achieve the position he held. Fortunately, it was during this same time that I had the privilege of becoming an adjunct instructor at Valley Forge Military College, a school known worldwide for its commitment to the development of ethics, character, and leadership. It is here that I had the opportunity to apply the principle of "maintaining a healthy dissatisfaction for the way things are." Without identifying the boss—and I use that term loosely—I was able to exploit his weaknesses as examples to the class on "how not to do things." I found that there was, after all, a silver lining to the cloud. We should learn from everyone we encounter, the good and the bad. The truly successful learn from adversity. Many have prospered greatly in the wake of disaster. They were learners and leaders. Donald Trump, for example, returned from near bankruptcy to considering a run for the presidency.

The customer is always right. We've heard that saying for years. It just so happens that it's true. One of the golden rules is "he with the gold makes the rules." While teaching TQM, I conducted an informal poll. Of the vast majority of the students who had made a large purchase within the past year, a new car, for example, had purchased from a dealer who had a reputation for quality service. This fact was more important to the customer than price. This demonstrates very clearly that we, as customers, demand and are entitled to proper service and are willing to seek it out. If we don' t service our customers, someone else will. If we don' t service them properly, we won't get repeat business or referrals. The customer defines quality! Companies must focus on meeting customer needs and expectations. It's as simple as that.

Now with my private-sector career firmly established, I provide security consultations and conduct sophisticated investigations for law offices, a "Big Five" accounting firm, and major companies internationally. The vast majority of my business is repeat and referral. That is my definition of success. Repeat and referral business is the ultimate testimony to your skills or product and to your leadership style as well. I value the referral every bit as much as the revenue it generates.

As a service provider, you're part of a diversified field. Specialized training, customized evaluation, and customer-focused education will help you meet the needs of all your clients. Quality has no boundaries. Leaders know that a successful quality culture requires a sustained senior leadership commitment to flourish. Top leaders should involve themselves completely in quality activities. They set policy and strategy, review action plans, and evaluate progress. Additionally, they guide the integration of quality into their training programs. Evaluation of progress, along with recognition and reward of team members by supervisory personnel at all levels, is critically important. Dr. W. Edwards Deming (founder of the quality movement and civilian assistant to General MacArthur, who rebuilt postwar Japan) said, "Americans still care about quality. The country is full of intelligent, courageous people who would change if they only knew how."

Professional Development

Knowledge complements change. Education and training are the cornerstones of career development. This is the most logical place to begin the introduction of total quality. Quality subject areas should be included in all organizational training and education programs, formal and informal. Leaders, as teachers, should apply quality principles while they function as facilitators, team members, supervisors, and advisors, both in practice and as a method of supporting the training objectives. People learn from what they see. Lead by example!

Quality Service Criteria

Before embarking on your quality journey, you are going to need assistance charting your course. A good guide for your quality indoctrination and maintenance is the renowned Malcolm Baldrige National Quality Award. Congress established this award in 1987 in honor of Baldrige, who served as Secretary of Commerce from 1981 until his death. A staunch believer in quality, this award is his legacy. The criteria are concepts and core values in seven broad categories, including 28 items and 92 areas. Items are the major elements of an effective quality system, while areas explain the intent of the items.

A quick reference guide to the four basic elements of the quality service criteria framework is:

Driver:

Senior executive leaders are responsible for the continuing pursuit of improving organizational performance and customer satisfaction. Quality must be driven from the top.

System:

Well-designed and clearly articulated processes to ensure customer satisfaction as well as meeting performance and quality goals. All personnel must become familiar with the system.

Measures of progress:

Results-oriented basis for directing actions for providing increasing customer satisfaction and organizational performance. Feedback—measure progress and performance.

Goals:

Providing continuous improvement in customer satisfaction and relations. The organizational goals, i.e., the mission and vision, must clearly articulate a need for improvement.

Criteria Framework

The purpose of the criteria is to provide a guide or framework to assist the leader in raising performance standards and expectations and help the assessment, training, and planning functions. Here's how the criteria framework can help you.

Help organizational goals of mission accomplishment by becoming better focused, more efficient, and highly effective.

Demonstrate how different functions within the organization work together.

Facilitate communications by clarifying organizational requirements of the mission and quality expectations.

Improve the organization's operational performance.

Scoring the criteria

Items within the framework are scored. Use your score to find your baseline—where are you now and where you want to be in the future. There are three facets to the scoring system: approach, application, and results.

The approach is the methodology used to accomplish the needs addressed by the items.

The application is the way in which the approach is utilized.

The results are the outcomes and effects in accomplishing the purposes raised in the criteria.

The following is a summary of the seven steps used in the criteria.

Leadership

Leaders demonstrate their commitment to quality by being directly involved in quality efforts, as well as through their personal training and education. Leadership involvement is measurable by observing how quality is integrated within the organization and if operations are customer-driven. Ask yourself this: Is quality practiced throughout the organization? This answer will tell you just what the leadership commitment to quality is.

Professional Development

People are your organization's most important resource. Does your organization recognize the importance of people and assist workers in achieving their full potential? Are employees empowered to reach their performance and quality goals? Examine the environment: Is there a culture that builds trust, teamwork, and excellence? Does the working environment meet the needs of the employees? These questions will help you determine how your organization sees and utilizes the workforce.

Planning

How does your organization plan? Is quality integrated into the company's long- and short-term plans? Are improvement plans made to enhance performance and include mission performance goals? Are items included in your strategic planning to recognize the achievements of employees? These questions can help you in charting the course for a quality-oriented organization.

Client Satisfaction

Truly successful organizations consistently meet or exceed their clients' needs. They recognize that the "customer is always right." They also recognize that their clients demand and deserve service. Companies that deliver quality products and service seek and heed feedback from their clients. The mission and vision statements should be directed toward the delivery of high-quality performance and complete customer satisfaction.

Examination and Analysis

Feedback from clients and input from personnel should be collected and analyzed to determine the health of the product or service rendered. The data is used to improve operational performance. Ask, how can the data be utilized to increase performance? What about service and products? What was the impact on internal operations? These questions help you examine your ability to improve overall performance.

Research and Development

How does the organization assess its processes and those of its vendors? Is your organization seeking to improve service or product delivery by researching and developing better ways to deliver the service or enhance the serviceability of the product? Except for wine, things don' t improve by themselves. It takes careful planning and attention to detail.

Results

What were your results? Did things improve? To answer these questions, you need proof—evidence that services and products actually improved performance and client satisfaction. Measure the data received from your employees and that received from the client. Remember to seek honest feedback and constructive criticism covering the entire service or process. Collect, store, and use this data. Include it in your professional development programs. Share it throughout the organization so that all may benefit. Avoid repeating the same mistakes.

Summary

The leader recognizes the need for continuous improvement and takes positive steps to achieve improvement. The leader makes a plan for his or her professional development and develops training programs for subordinates. The leader establishes effective communications, seeks feedback, and recognizes the efforts of others. The quality leader is true to his principles and is loyal to the organization. He sets the example others are proud to emulate.

Leadership

Successful leaders provide continuing growth opportunities, as well as the tools and professional development needed to accomplish the vision and mission. Today's leaders recognize quality as a basic responsibility that can' t be delegated. Leaders understand that quality is leader-driven; it comes from the top. Quality isn' t new, only our expectations and demands for total quality are new. When American manufacturers had little or no international competition, we lost sight of quality. However, the post World War II industrial revolution awakened our understanding for the need for quality as well as our desire to receive quality products and services. Leaders communicate through their actions; they lead by example. Leaders clearly demonstrate and communicate what is taking place presently and what they see and expect for the future—that's the vision and mission.

Mission

The primary task of any organization is to perform its mission. Your mission statement should describe the tasks you face, your available resources, what you want to achieve, and your methods of operation. Your mission is your symbol— it represents who you are and outlines your goals. It is enduring and will stand for long periods of time. Everyone in the organization must understand and adhere to the mission as a prerequisite for success. People perform the mission, and the mission comes first.

Vision

The vision statement is a presentation of your picture of the future. A vision is what you want to become as an organization. As the mission statement describes your business, the vision statement determines your path and helps you determine what' s important. Vision is a slow process that you will work toward every day.

People are the key ingredient. Proud, hard-working, talented, and well-trained people are your key to total success. Your past is your foundation; build upon it. Your people are instrumental in laying the groundwork connecting the past with the future. Following the vision gives them the map and provides them with the inspiration and guidance needed to accomplish the mission.

Quality Culture

The style, principles, and values define your organization. Your culture defines you, what you stand for, and how you operate. True leaders strive to create an operational environment or culture based on values and principles that provide a cohesive and productive organization. Leaders at all levels help by ensuring cooperation.

Ethics

Professional ethics is important to each of us as individuals and as professionals. We must strive to live by the highest ethical standards if we are to maintain trust and retain effectiveness. In most day-to-day activities, the basic code of behavior that you learned from your family, friends, and peers (the golden rule) guides you to act in an ethical manner. However, ethics is more than a rigid set of rules for behavior; rather, personal judgment is needed to decide complex ethical issues.

The United States is increasingly concerned with ethics. More and more professors are teaching courses in ethics than ever before. Professional groups—doctors, lawyers, engineers, business managers, and others— are setting codes of ethical standards for their groups. As citizens, we are obligated to honor constitutional justice, civil law, and the social and ethnic mores of our communities.

At the moment of decision making or action taking, the professional is crowded with signals emanating from rule-oriented demands, goal-oriented obligations, and situation-oriented challenges. Each individual is responsible for balancing the moral claims of these sources and for determining which signals merit priority. Military and public safety personnel, more than most, live under a sense of obligation, aligned with a strong sense of discipline, order, and obedience. Dilemmas exist when two or more obligations conflict. How we handle these dilemmas and conflicts will define our personal leadership style. This is the time to be hailed as being honest, fair, courageous, and steadfast in your resolve.

Human needs are a leader's prevailing problem and, accordingly, a leader's top priority. Take care of your people and they will take care of you. People have needs, they have frailties, and they all have potential. People deserve recognition, consideration, and encouragement. People should be the focus of every command and the heart of every mission.

Values are the core of your proud foundation and are essential to your future as well as that of your organization. Honor, integrity, courage, skill, and tenacity are the major characteristics that define the successful culture.

Honor is perhaps the embodiment of the sum of the personal commitment, and loyalty values we all treasure—integrity, courage, loyalty, honesty, and pride.

Integrity is probably the second major ethical concern for leaders. Integrity is the commitment to honesty and fair play that provides the foundation for trust. Demonstrated integrity helps build Quality as well as credibility with internal and external customers. In high-threat environments, integrity is a life-critical element of every job along the way. Dishonesty can only be reversed if key professionals insist on honor and exemplify integrity. Former General Electric chief Jack Welch commenting on integrity, said, "Integrity is the rock upon which we build our business success—our quality products and services, our forthright relations with customers and suppliers, and ultimately, our winning competitive record. GE's quest for competitive excellence begins and ends with our commitment to ethical conduct."

Courage provides the moral strength, the backbone, to do the right thing regardless of the consequences. Courage is the critical element in long-term improvement! Courage is the ability to fight the temptation to take shortcuts and make temporary repairs. Courage has special significance when empowering others. It is easy to help others succeed, it takes courage to let them fail and learn from their mistakes.

Skill is the trademark of the master craftsman. Leaders build their knowledge, experience, and competence as an ongoing evolution. They learn from others as well as from their own experience. They seek opportunities to learn through formal and informal sources. Dr. Martin Luther King said, "If you' re going to be a janitor, be the best janitor you can be." Whatever your job, be the best; become an expert.

Persistence or tenacity is the determination to continue. Winners don't quit and quitters don't win. Quality organizations have a corporate value of tenacity, they watch for obstacles that can impede progress. They overcome obstacles and impediments.

Commitment engenders client satisfaction. The client who senses your commitment to their cause is likely to be both a satisfied and repeat customer. A quality culture provides an environment where clients' needs are anticipated and met. Client needs come first.

Loyalty is recognition of the importance of the vision and mission. Leaders often sacrifice for the greater good. Leaders are indeed people dedicated to something bigger than themselves. Doing what is best for the client, organization, and co-workers is ultimately what is best for you.

Principles are the support for the core values. They are a promise or commitment to the values and provide guidance in achieving your goals. Personal involvement, dedication, respect, empowerment, and leadership-by-fact are the guidelines for your operating style.

Personal Involvement is establishing the example, mission, vision, policy, procedures, priorities, and strategies. Leaders communicate these actions through word and deed; they create an environment that supports values.

Dedication to the vision and mission is represented in the strength of the team.

Respect for the institution and the individual takes place when you appreciate the vision and mission and recognize everyone' s efforts and contributions toward mission and vision accomplishment. Place value on everyone and their role in the organization. Don't let position or influences serve as your only guidelines for respect.

Empowerment provides your most valuable resource, people, with the tools, authority, responsibility, and opportunity they need to do the job. Empowerment is not about relinquishing power it has nothing to do with power. Its about allowing people to do what they were hired to do—their jobs. Leaders who understand the value of empowerment soon learn that their role has been strengthened, not weakened.

Leadership By Fact utilizes measurements, information, and data to indicate who, what, when, where, why, and how to proceed. Data supported decisions help you eliminate emotion from the decision making process. These fact-based decisions will lead to a smarter, fairer, and more productive way of conducting business.

Your Leadership Style

Put the basics of quality values and principles to work. Let them help you and your organization achieve success. This is an important role in changing your workplace environment and culture. Your personal behaviors and example create a distinctive and easily recognized leadership style. Let yours be positive. You only have one chance to make a first impression.

Create an environment that emphasizes values and principles. Inspire teamwork and trust; instill pride and a sense of performance ownership. Recognize and reward the accomplishments of the individual, the team, and the organization. This promotes professionalism.

Recognize and appreciate that a subordinate can only serve one superior effectively. "Too many cooks spoil the soup" and too many superiors send conflicting messages. Don't add to the confusion. Provide clear direction and unity of control.

Don't shy away from delegating jobs that can be stressful. Obviously, too much stress can be damaging, but on the other hand, growth isn't likely in a job without stress. Delegate to the lowest effective level within the organization. This provides challenge for the upwardly mobile and frees up the supervisor who tends to do it all himself. Delegate assignments and empower individuals and teams to complete the assignments. Provide them with the tools, support, training, and recognition, and they will readily accept accountability for the results. You will be pleased with the outcome.

Set goals and measure progress. Use facts and data to support your findings. Reward people for their accomplishments. Retrain them when they fail; effectively communicate the objectives and appropriate procedures. Remember to praise in public and condemn in private. This form of training is discipline in its truest and most effective form.

Empower the people who are doing the job. Let them have a stake in the outcome. Pride in ownership is a tremendous motivator. Think of it as an artist signing a painting—people want their name associated with success. Put their names on the "painting." Give credit where it's due.

Challenge everyone to improve. Commenting on challenge during his infamous speech on June 5, 1944, General George S. Patton said, "When you here, every one of you, were kids, you all admired the champion marble player, the fastest runner, the toughest boxer, the big league ball players, and the All-American football players. Americans love a winner. Americans will not tolerate a loser. Americans despise cowards. Americans play to win all of the time...." We all need to be challenged, for without challenge, there can be no reward. Learn and understand your client's needs. There is no room or time for "business as usual." We need to do the job bigger, smarter, faster, and better the first time. Ask yourself and your colleagues this question: how come there is never enough time to do things right the first time, but always enough time to fix it later?

Summary

These values and principles of leadership have stood the test of time. We have seen where they have been eroded—in failed organizations and trashed careers everywhere. There are no substitutes for correct behavior! Your vision, mission, culture, actions, and operations must demonstrate a solid commitment to values and principles. Without values and principles, we are reduced to something less than what we envision for ourselves and for our organization and something far less than what is desired or deserved by our customers.

Your Role in Quality

Where do you start? First, you must make a total commitment to becoming a Quality Leader. Prepare yourself for leadership; think about leadership, study leadership, and practice leadership.

Senior leaders point the direction for the organization. Senior leaders depend on the most experienced members of the organization for assistance in setting the pace. Identifying the organization' s values, mission, and vision are the critical first steps. Senior leaders evaluate the organization's values to determine future needs. They work hard on strategic planning. Planning could consume as much as 70 percent of the executive' s time. This is time well spent. It is the senior leaders who are ultimately responsible for where the organization is and where it's going. In addition to planning, senior leaders interface with clients, they concentrate on projects that complement the vision and mission, and evaluate progress toward goals using objective measuring tools.

Top administrators understand the importance of creating both short-term (12–24 months) and long-range plans (3+ years) often referred to as the "five-year plan." The organization uses these plans to stay on track for the long term. These plans are created to benefit the organization and should survive changes in leadership. However, it is prudent to anticipate the need to make mid-course adjustments to accommodate changes in personnel and operational requirements.

Leaders communicate. They listen. They actively seek feedback from both internal and external customers. Why? Communication is an absolutely critical element to success. Leaders must evaluate progress and improvement. They need to know if the organization is true to its vision, mission, values, and principles. Effective communication assists both leaders and workers to better understand what works best and what the customer wants and needs.

Cooperation! Leaders create a culture of communication, cooperation, and coordination. They do this by establishing policies and procedures, and by providing the tools that enable and empower people to do their jobs within the structure of the vision, mission, values, and principles of the organization. They recognize the importance and contributions of every man, every unit, and every department in the organization. They build teams!

Mid-level leaders. Previously thought of as managers, and supervisors, the mid-level leader is the on-site expert. The day-to-day "boss" with the most personal contact with workers. The mid-level leader should be the teacher, mentor, and coach. These leaders provide the training and tools to get the job done. They provide encouragement and they support the quality improvement processes and programs. They ensure compliance with the vision, mission, values, and operational procedures of the organization. Mid-level managers measure performance and improvement. They collect data and information and apply it to quality-improvement issues.

Communication here, as at all levels, is critical. The successful leader clearly articulates information, data, procedures, policies, and programs. The leader ensures everyone both up and down the organizational chart understands "how are we doin'?" Chief among communications is the effective establishment of two-way communication—everyone needs to be clear on the organization's vision, mission, values, and principles. When leaders are trusted, communication improves. Workers who know the most generally do the best job. Solicit feedback and be open to suggestions.

Individuals. Everyone is an individual; respect that fact. In a quality organization, individuals are the experts. Their skills and input are critical to continuous improvement. Everyone in the organization must learn the plans, goals, and processes that provide the clients with the best services and products. They also need to understand each other's contributions to overall operations. They need to become part of the team. Without team effort, without them, there can be no true success. Everyone needs to know and practice the company vision and mission. Everyone serves the whole.

Your organization has people who deal directly with clients. They probably know better than anyone does what it takes to satisfy the client. These workers can't meet organizational goals without understanding the processes. Provide these frontline employees with training programs. Include them in discussions and make them members of teams that affect production. Have them share their knowledge of the clients' likes and dislikes, needs and desires. Involve them in evaluating the products, services, and programs that affect their clients. Get individuals involved! They can serve an important role in assisting in the evolution of the vision, mission, and planning.

Treat everyone with dignity and respect. Celebrate their worth and watch them flourish. Apply the other golden rule—"treat others as you would be treated."

Summary

Leadership at all levels is the key to establishing the organization as a winner. Leadership is the power behind the organization. Leaders provide the support, compassion, skills, knowledge, and values that serve as the guide for the group. Individuals look to the leader for guidance and follow his example. Accordingly, the leader must always behave in a manner that brings credit upon himself, his profession, and his organization. The leader does the right thing and accepts nothing less of others. Leaders revel in the success of others.

The Basics

Take care of your people. As a leader, you have been given a precious gift, the responsibility of caring for others. Handle this responsibility first, foremost, and always! Remember Maslow's hierarchy of needs. Maslow stated that there are five primary levels on the ladder of human motivation, they are:

- Biological needs – Bodily needs always come first.
- Safety needs – People will not feel free to produce until their safety and security needs have been met.
- Social needs – Once the physical needs have been met, people need and want to have a sense of belonging.
- Esteem needs – Commonly thought of as ego. People desire and deserve recognition for their efforts.
- Need for self-actualization – This is self-satisfaction, the confidence of the individual to recognize that they have made it—they have become successful.

You as the leader must provide the tools, means, support, encouragement, and environment for workers to achieve these five levels of needs. Once provided to your subordinates, you will have also made it to number five because that should be your goal toward self-satisfaction.

Experience tells us that certain things have to happen in order to lead effectively. We all have been exposed to a "boss" that has caused us to question what is happening or why. Over the years, we have all heard about basic supervisory techniques—well, they're as valid today as when you first heard them. Use them; they work.

The basic elements of organizational socialization – Everyone, superiors and subordinates alike, needs to understand these basic things in order to become successful and productive:

- The basic GOALS of the organization
- The preferred MEANS by which those goals should be attained
- The basic RESPONSIBILITIES of the member in his/her assigned role
- The BEHAVIOR PATTERNS which are required for effective performance in the role
- A set of RULES or PRINCIPLES, which pertain to the maintenance of the identity and integrity of the organization

Assess capabilities – Look carefully and objectively at your subordinates' capabilities. Provide tasks that are challenging, yet within their limits. Maximum growth and professional development happen when people are required to work to the limit, but have the support, training, and motivation to get the job done.

Provide feedback – Feedback must be constructive, timely, and accurate. To be effective, feedback should be balanced (both positive and negative) and personal but never a personal attack. Remember, praise in public and condemn in private.

Be concise and consistent about what is expected. Clearly outline the five Ws: who, what, when, where, and why—and don't forget how. Be specific— most problems develop from a failure to communicate. If you're not sure, ask. Confirm that your instructions are understood. Then let your people know that you are confident that they can and will achieve the desired results.

Don't expect immediate perfection. Even you weren't perfect at first. One of the most important functions of a leader is preparing subordinates to grow to the fullest extent possible. Surely you've heard the recruiting jingles of the U.S. military: "Be all that you can be..." "Aim High, Aim Air Force," "Be Part of the Few, the Proud, the Marines." The military has long known something that private business is finally recognizing: it is the responsibility of the organization to provide for professional development opportunities. Help your people be all they can be, have them set their sights on greater opportunity, and watch their pride of accomplishment.

Know how to maintain professional relations with personnel. Being friendly, rather than friends at work helps maintain relationships. Over-familiarity is the breading ground of contempt. It undermines the authority of the superior and can be detrimental to the subordinate as well. Common courtesy, manners, and a pleasant disposition are a winning combination. Remember three key words to a successful relationship – please and thank you. While serving as a football coach at West Point, Vince Lombardi said, "the test of this century is whether we mistake growth of wealth and power for growth in strength and character. We've weakened discipline and respect for authority and let the freedom of the individual predominate." Treat superiors and subordinates alike with dignity and respect.

Appearance, grooming, and physical fitness – The adage that we are often judged by the appearance we make is absolutely true. Also true is the saying "you only get one chance to make a first impression." Many professions still adhere to strict standards of appearance. Many others maintain an informal dress code. Imagine taking your legal or financial business to a firm where there is no attention to the attire and appearance of its employees. Picture two automotive repair shops—one is clean and neat, reminiscent of a hospital; the other is filthy and the service technicians are in dirty clothes and they are poorly groomed. Tools and equipment are scattered about—it isn't a stretch to think you would take your car to the former. People are taken more seriously and have greater inherent credibility when they present in a professional fashion. Professionals pay attention to details. Stay away from the trendy fashions. Attila, King of the Huns, said, "Chieftains are as they appear to their Huns."

Health and fitness go hand in hand. As much as we want to deny it, we all look at and evaluate others. The physical characteristics of a person are measured every bit as much as their attire and grooming. Additionally, physically fit people are likely to be more energetic and have greater endurance. They are also likely to be healthier and be absent less from the workplace. They feel better physically and about themselves. Fitness builds confidence. An analogy similar to the automotive repair shops can be made with people—perhaps sometimes unfair, but true. Attila commenting on physical stamina, said, "...a healthy body supports a health mind...chieftains cannot lead from their bedsides..."

Summary

Look and act the part. Successful leaders lead by example in appearance and performance. Set the rules by your actions; "actions speak louder than words." Respect yourself, the organization, your profession, and everyone with whom you come into contact and the respect will be reciprocal. Seek and accept the suggestions and input of others. Recognize and reward the efforts of others, up and down the organization. Have a good word for others. Set the standards high; you can' t achieve greatness if you seek mediocrity. Maintain professional development, exhibit pride, aim high, and everyone can become successful.

Common Qualities of Good Leaders

Be a good follower. To be a good leader, you must start at the beginning and learn how to be a good follower. Follow the old Navy adage that you should have loyalty up as well as loyalty down. All good leaders know that regardless of your position in life, you will always have a senior. You must be loyal to that senior. As a member of an organization, you must be loyal to that organization. Be the kind of dynamic subordinate that you would have working with you.

All organizations are filled with subordinates, but few of us get much basic survival training for that role, not to mention training on how we might make those roles dynamic, synergistic, and satisfying.

Our success in effectively filling our subordinate roles is the key to our present security as well as to our future promotion and success. In order for us to be dynamic in our positions we must know what the job is and how to do it. The subordinate must know precisely what the boss expects. The more ambiguity there is in the job, the more likely there is to be confusion and confusion is the breading ground for problems. It is the subordinate's responsibility to initiate discussions with the boss to clear up any misunderstandings. Again, if you don't know, ask questions! The subordinate must clearly understand his role and what is expected of him. One unyielding requirement for subordinates is to evaluate themselves and their skills in relation to what the tasks require. Do the job! That's what the boss expects and that's what you get paid for. That is what will lead to success. Become the trusted adviser to whom the boss comes to get the straight information. Dynamic subordinates will be alert to ways they can rescue their boss from mistakes of commission and omission. Invite feedback and provide feedback. Be accountable, share responsibility, and build trust.

Seek Responsibility

Fine leaders seek responsibility. They have an attitude of "somebody has got to be in charge and it might as well be me." They thoroughly enjoy getting worthwhile things accomplished. They readily accept the increased risks and accountability associated with exercising greater authority. They are competitive individuals, possessing high degrees of pride, and satisfy that pride in achieving productive ends. They are fighters with a strong will to win.

Relate well to others. Successful leaders have strong people skills. They are aware of people and know how to relate well to others. They make a point of learning about their subordinates, their backgrounds, their likes and dislikes, and such. They seem to have a special skill for mentally retaining their knowledge about their subordinates. As they move from assignment to assignment, they reach into that "file" and seek to have some of those fine people work for them. Surround yourself with good people and inspire them to do their best.

Intelligence

Most leaders are also intelligent. This is more difficult to describe. Certainly, intelligence entails possessing a wealth of knowledge, but more important, intelligence connotes the ability to perceive what is important. You will find that most good leaders can look at confusing situations and complex details and quickly analyze the key issues. They never fall prey to the tendency to become too busy with the urgent to forget the important. Observe wisely the occurrences around you and learn from them. Have broad interests and seek to develop a diversified base of knowledge that will enable you to establish the relative value and importance of events. Read extensively, avail yourself of educational and training opportunities. Stay current with technical developments. Know your stuff and know your job. Technical skill and professional competence has a profound effect on your leadership ability. Knowledge is power.

Stamina

Successful leaders possess a high level of stamina. They have the ability to keep themselves going for long periods of time. They seem tireless and have very positive mental outlooks. Outstanding leaders are also tenacious—they don' t quit in the face of adversity. Physical health and well-being are critical to success. Look at the military as an example where all leaders are required to be physically in shape and they are subject to annual physical examinations. Follow this example, stay in shape and see your doctor regularly—it will pay off.

Moral Courage

Perhaps the most important quality I have observed in outstanding leaders is moral courage— to know right from wrong, to possess a firm set of values, and to live by those values and do what is right regardless of the consequences. There is strength in truth and accuracy. The true leader lives by a high standard of honor in every aspect of his life.

To prove a point, consider what Attila, King of the Huns, said regarding the qualities of leadership nearly 2000 years ago. Attila is generally considered to have been a barbarian; however, despite widespread fear of his savagery, Attila was a just ruler. Compare his innermost thoughts on leadership to those we hold true in today's enlightened leadership styles:

- Loyalty: ...above all things, a Hun must be loyal.
- Courage: ...chieftains who lead our Huns must be courageous.
- Desire: ...weak is the chieftain who does not want to be one.
- Emotional stamina: ...we must ensure that leaders at every level have the stamina to recover quickly from disappointment.
- Physical stamina: ...Huns must have chieftains who can endure the physical demands of their leadership duties.
- Empathy: ...chieftains must develop an understanding and appreciation of the values of others, sensitivity for other cultures, beliefs, and traditions.
- Decisiveness: ...vacillation and procrastination confuse and discourage subordinates, peers, and superiors and serve the enemy well.
- Anticipation: ...learning by observation and instincts honed by experience.
- Timing: ...one often develops this skill by applying lessons learned through failure.
- Competitiveness: ...a leader without a sense of competitiveness is easily overcome by the slightest challenge.
- Self-confidence: ...proper training and experience develops a personal feeling of assurance.
- Accountability: ...chieftains must never heap praise or lay blame on others for what they themselves achieve or fail to accomplish, no matter how grave or glorious the consequences.
- Responsibility: ...no king, chieftain, or subordinate should ever be allowed to serve who will not accept full responsibility for his actions.
- Credibility: ...leaders lacking in credibility will not gain proper influence and are to be hastily removed from positions of responsibility, for they cannot be trusted.

- Tenacity: ...the quality of unyielding drive to accomplish assignments is a desirable and essential quality of leadership.
- Dependability: ...if a chieftain cannot be depended upon in all situations to carry out his roles and responsibilities, relieve him of them.
- Stewardship: ...leaders must have a caretaker quality—they must encourage confidence, trust, and loyalty. Subordinates are not to be abused; they are to be guided, developed, and rewarded for their performance.

Two thousand years of human evolution and countless studies on the qualities of great leaders, and essentially nothing has changed.

Summary

The great football coach Vince Lombardi stated, "Character, not education, is man's greatest need and man's greatest safeguard. For character is higher than intellect. The real difference between men is in their character and in their energy, in the strong will and the skilled purpose." Practice dynamic subordinacy and learn how to lead by learning how to follow. Leading by example means that your honor, virtue, integrity, honesty, and courage are open for examination. Others will be watching. Don't compromise your ethics for the "quick fix" or any other reason. Find the "right way" and encourage others by your actions. Think of others and think about the consequences before you act. Think, ask, plan, and then act!

Communications

The importance of effective communications cannot be overstated. Communications is a critical element to the survival, let alone the success of every organization. At sometime and in some way, it is likely that ALL problems can be identified with, if not directly attributed to, poor communication. In 1938 Chester Barnard concluded that "communications was the main task of managers and executives." Well, it hasn't changed!

Communication must be both up and down the chain of command and throughout the organization. It is important for subordinates and superiors alike to keep each other informed. The first step in improving communications in your organization is to provide a good working environment. Communications should be objective, clear, articulate, and constructive. Things of a personally derogatory nature have no place in professional communications. Common sense, common decency, and common courtesy must prevail. Personal attacks serve only to hurt both individuals involved and ultimately the organization.

Encourage Feedback

Remember what Ed Koch asked: "How am I doin'"? If you don't ask, you won't know. Seek feedback from clients, customers (internal and external), co-workers, superiors, and subordinates. Provide feedback to the same list. Encourage and provide both good and bad news. Encourage constructive criticism and professional disagreement on issues. Identify areas where you want and need feedback. Use silence to promote feedback—don't interrupt. Watch for non-verbal clues— body language speaks volumes. Consider scheduling feedback sessions—planned feedback sessions often get more response than an impulsive "how are things going?"

Achieve Group Consensus

One of the biggest problems a supervisor faces is getting the group to reach consensus. Of course there are times when you must make an independent decision and stick to it. Frequently, policy decisions are made in the give and take of small-group discussions. Problem solving is a major goal of decision-making groups at all levels. Without consensus, morale and organizational satisfaction will likely suffer. With genuine consensus, an organization tends to embrace, support, and implement new policies. Communication, discussion, and debate aren't arguments. You can't win an argument. Dale Carnegie, in his world-renowned course, advises, "You can't win an argument. You can't because if you lose it, you lose it; and if you win it, you lose it. Why? Well, suppose you triumph over the other man and shoot his argument full of holes and prove that he is non compos mentis. Then what? You will feel fine, but what about him? You have made him feel inferior. You have hurt his pride. He will resent your triumph. And '…a man convinced against his will, is of the same opinion still.'"

Clarify the Discussion

Ensure that the group's activity is understandable, orderly, and focused on one issue at a time. Consensus comes more easily when each of the factors is weighed individually and systematically.

Use process statements. Group process or dynamics deals with such things as norms, cohesiveness, individual roles, group feelings, and needs. Process statements serve to stimulate and facilitate conversation. "What you've said seems to make sense. How do the rest of you feel?" or "So far, we seem to agree on the first two points; let's move on to the third" or "Have we heard from Bill?" Questions that seek clarification and encourage feedback serve to enhance communications. When the leader and group members use process statements effectively, agreement will come more readily and satisfaction will be increased.

Seek different views and remain open to those views. All persons should be encouraged to participate and express their points of view. All input has value. Allow participants to present their views and the evidence supporting their view. Expression of a wide range of opinions and positions allows an opportunity for learning to take place. Good leaders often learn from their subordinates. Leaders can serve as models for the behavior of others by not being overly opinionated. Studies have shown that low or moderately opinionated supervisors are held in higher esteem than highly opinionated ones.

Use group pronouns. Less effective groups tend to use self-referent or indulgent words, such as I, me, my, and mine. Cohesive, effective, and successful groups tend to use group referent words, such as we, ours, and us. As a leader, talk about the group and group members. Emphasize the achievements of the group and of the individuals. Talk about what we hope to achieve and how we can work together. Praise the group and individuals; give them the credit.

Conflict Resolution

For a leader to manage conflict, it is imperative to understand its source. The three basic sources of conflict are semantic, role, and values.

Semantic sources. These are the conflicts generated by a communication failure, the failure of two individuals to share fully the meaning of a communicative attempt.

Role sources. These conflicts arise from the assorted perceptions of people about their expected behaviors or the expectations of others. Role conflicts may be evidenced in those situations in which the boss and subordinate seem to be butting heads because each perceives the role of the other in a reference frame different from observable behavior—they don't see what they think they see.

Value sources. These conflicts are based upon the individualistic value sets of people. These value sets readily contribute to differences between people because people are different. Every individual is just that, an individual and they cause us at times, to respond or behave in an unexpected fashion because we are behaving according to our value set and not that of the others. Managing value conflicts requires an awareness of other people' s values and a capacity to adapt to those situations. What is effective in one situation may not be in the next. Consideration and courtesy are the keys to adapting to individual values.

Most people believe that the prime cause of conflict is ineffective communication. Differences in value and rule sets are most likely to be the cause of ineffective communication and therefore the most likely source of conflict. The motivation of separate individuals is an additional leading source of conflict. A third major cause of conflict is the differing ideals and philosophical bases we all posses.

Conflict can have both positive and negative effects. It can be positive when it encourages creativity and constructive input. Conflict is negative when it establishes turmoil in interpersonal or organizational relations, fosters distrust, creates resistance to change, builds a feeling of defeat or hopelessness, or adds to misunderstanding. All conflict is not bad. There will be times when a leader would want to use stimulating conflict to encourage creativity and feedback. Properly harnessed, conflict can be a valuable management tool.

Conflict resolution requires that the parties in conflict trust each other and that the parties in conflict are capable and willing to identify the source of the conflict and then objectively deal with it. Repressing conflict, or "sweeping it under the rug," does nothing to eliminate the source. Repressing conflict is potentially as damaging as the conflict itself because the conflict will most likely manifest and resurface. As a general rule, a decision not to address the conflict is probably wrong. Treat the disease, not the symptom.

A frequently used method for resolving conflict is the use of the subordinate's goals. The manager shows how the conflict is reducing productivity, thus reducing benefits to the individual. A unique way of resolving conflict is to increase the interaction between conflicting individuals and groups. Remember the adage about walking a mile in someone else's shoes. Having conflicting groups and individuals understand each other's perspective is effective in conflict resolution. The result should be better communication, greater understanding, and less future conflict. Basic to efforts to reduce or resolve conflict is the idea of avoiding win-lose situations.

Summary

Studies by the International Association of Business Communication and interviews of chief executives of fifty major U.S. and Canadian corporations revealed that "face-to-face communications, including group meetings and one-to-one dialogue" was the most important and effective way to communicate with employees. Furthermore, most executives believe that there is a positive relationship between effective communication and employee productivity. The primary responsibility for communication in any organization rests with those in leadership positions. The successful leader works hard to prevent communication bottlenecks and resolve conflict through effective communication. Communicate up, down, and throughout.

Quotes: When in doubt you can depend on the classics.

"To see what is right and not do it is want of courage." Confucius, 551–479 B.C.

"'Tis true, that we are in great danger; the greater therefore should our courage be." Shakespeare: *King Henry V*.
_____*Profiles in Courage*, 1955.

"Communications dominate war; broadly considered, they are the most important single element in strategy, political or military." Mahan: *The Problem of Asia*, 1900.

"Respect yourself and others will respect you." Confucius, 551–479 B.C.

"The superior man is firm in the right way, and not merely firm." Confucius, 551–479 B.C.

"He that ruleth over men must be just." *II Samuel, XXIII.*

"Self-confidence is the first requisite to great undertakings." Samuel Johnson, *Lives of the Poets*, 1779.

"This world belongs to the energetic." R.W. Emerson, 1803–1882.

"Trust men, and they will be true to you." R.W. Emerson, 1803–1882.

"Loyalty is the marrow of honor." Paul von Hindenburg, *Out of My Life*, 1920.

"There is a great deal of talk about loyalty from the bottom to the top. Loyalty from the top down is even more necessary and much less prevalent." George S. Patton, *War As I Knew It*, 1947

"My honor is dearer to me than my life." Cervantes, *Don Quixote*, 1604.

"If I lose my honor, I lose myself." Shakespeare, *Anthony & Cleopatra*, 1606.

"Keep honor, like your sabre, bright, Shame coward fear—and then if we must perish in the fight, Oh! Let us die like men." George Washington Patten, 1808–1882.

"Tenacity of purpose and untiring energy in execution can repair a first mistake and baffle deeply laid plans." Alfred Thayer Mahan, 1840–1914.

"Victory will come to the side that outlasts the other." Ferdinand Foch, September 1914.

In Conclusion

Managing Client Expectations: The Cost of Dissatisfied Customers

A study by *Fortune* magazine and the Forum Corporation discovered the following:

- Satisfied clients will tell an average of five other people about their positive experiences with a company's service or product.
- The dissatisfied client on average will tell niine other people about a negative experience with a company's service or product.
- But 13 percent of dissatisfied customers will tell twenty or more people about their negative experience with a company's performance.
- Worst of all, 98 percent of dissatisfied customers never complain; they just go to a competitor.

The White House Office of Consumer Affairs reports: "An unhappy customer remembers the incident for 23.5 years and talks about it for 18 months."

We as service professionals must be alert for the signs of a dissatisfied client and ALWAYS make it right. Our reputations and our businesses are at stake. Do it right, or next time someone else will get the job!

Acknowledgments

I don' t want to be remembered solely for my accomplishments, but rather as someone who is truly grateful for all the love, help, support, and guidance he received from family, friends, and colleagues. This book, as well as any of my other accomplishments, wouldn't have been possible without them. This book is dedicated to my family and friends; my parents, who instilled in me a sense of purpose and patriotism; and my wife and best friend, Alice, who has always been there— through thick and thin, good times and bad, shift work, missed holidays, danger, and separations, all without complaint.

My parents: Mom and Dad, thanks for laying the groundwork!

My wife, Alice: The inspiration behind and the foundation of every success!

My son, Chuck: Honest and straightforward without exception—in a world of compromise, some men don't!

My mentors: Tom Gallagher: Pride, integrity, and courage above all else!

General Bob Harris: Nice guys don't finish last—the perfect example of a professional and a gentleman!

Colonel Don Rowe: The true meaning of education and understanding!

Time and space prohibit mentioning everyone who has been there for me. Believe me, I truly appreciate everything you've done for me. It is my hope that my gratitude will be evident in the level of professionalism I bring to my trade.

Thank you one and all!

About the Author

Charles Read has more than two decades of extensive and diverse military and law enforcement experience. As a Chief of Security Police within the elite Air Force Special Operations Command, his responsibility was operational command of all aspects of airbase security and law enforcement. He led security deployments in support of special operations missions in England, Honduras, Puerto Rico, Japan, Korea, and Saudi Arabia. During the Persian Gulf War (the Saudi deployment), he served as the Senior Security Adviser for AFSOC (Air Force Special Operations Command). During his tenure with the New York State Police and Pennsylvania Bureau of Criminal Investigation, he conducted complex investigations, including major frauds, organized crime, homicide, and fugitives. He has also served in the Governor's Protection Detail, special patrol, and training units.

Read is a Certified Fraud Consultant, a licensed private detective, and a Certified Security Consultant. He has received a degree from the University of the State of New York and is a graduate of the Pennsylvania State University Police Executive Development Institute. He has served as a certified arbitrator for the Better Business Bureau and as an instructor of Criminal Justice, the Dynamics of Terrorism, and Leadership Development at Valley Forge Military College.

Memberships include the Fraternal Order of Police, the International Association of Chiefs of Police, VIDOCQ Society, and the National Council of Investigation & Security Services. Read has received numerous civilian and military commendations and awards for outstanding public service, including the Federal Executive Board "Excellence in Government Award."

Read established his private practice in 1993 and is the founder and director of ISI Consulting located in Duck, North Carolina. ISI provides a wide range of risk management and security consulting services to select clients in business, industry, and government.

Recognizing the need to increase professionalism within the private security field, Read joined the faculty of the Lion Investigation Academy (LIA) and developed the Certified Security Consultant program. The information presented in this book is largely based upon material developed for that course.

Praise for
Principles of Security Consulting

"Comprehensive and well presented. The Lion Investigation Academy has adopted Principles of Security Consulting as the required text for the award of the Certified Security Consultant designation. Don' t even think of entering the Security Consulting business unless you read this book."
– Joseph Alercia, II, JD BCFE, CMI; Founder & CEO, Lion Investigation Academy; President, American Detective Agency

"Well presented, comprehensive, and most informative. I plan to introduce it to my Security Management and Criminal Justice students at John Jay College of Criminal Justice as well as to the sworn personnel of the Sea Gate Police Department. Anyone serious about a professional Security of Public Safety career should read this book."
– Robert Abraham, Chief of Police, Sea Gate, NY; Inspector (retired) NYPD; Professor of Criminal Justice, John Jay College, CUNY.

"Charlie Read, whose law enforcement and private sector security experience is exceptionally broad, now presents a 'must have' addition to any law enforcement or security professional's library. Never before has there been such synthesis of topical material in one place. This book provides unique insight and perspective for both novices and seasoned practitioners. At a time when an assured security presence is of foremost concern in virtually every sector of civilized society, in boardrooms as well as bedrooms, this work is both timely and of momentous practical value. No competent security consultant should be without it."
– Michael J. Hawley, Esquire